TO BE FREE

We are all of one race: human.

TO BE FREE

understanding and eliminating racism

THOMAS PEACOCK
MARLENE WISURI

Foreword by Eric Jolly

afton press

THE PUBLICATION OF

TO BE FREE
understanding and eliminating racism

and its distribution to
selected Minnesota schools
has been made possible
by major gifts from:

TARGET
and
TRAVELERS

with additional generous gifts from

Katherine B. Andersen Fund of
The Saint Paul Foundation

Fred C. and Katherine B.
Andersen Foundation

F. R. Bigelow Foundation

Blandin Foundation

Boss Foundation

Jud Dayton

William and Bonnie Frels

Grotto Foundation

Willis C. Helm Family Fund of
The Minneapolis Foundation

Home Federal Savings Bank

Huss Foundation

James Johnson

Malcolm and Patricia McDonald

Quaker Hill Foundation

Margaret Rivers Fund

The Saint Paul Foundation

Walker Foundation

Wells Fargo Bank, N.A.
Rochester, Minnesota

Ted and Nancy Weyerhaeuser

Weyerhaeuser Foundation

also: Brad and Mary Louise Clary
Jake and Angel Crandall
Andy Currie
Lucy Rosenberry Jones

as well as many other friends!

FRONT COVER: Parade Day by Ray Caron, oil on canvas,
photograph by Chuck Johnston.
BACK COVER: Kids with Globe by Polka Dot Images.

Edited by Ashley Shelby
Designed by Mary Susan Oleson
Production assistance by Beth Williams
Printed by Pettit Network Inc., Afton, Minnesota

Library of Congress Cataloging-in-Publication Data
Peacock, Thomas.
  To be free / by Thomas Peacock and Marlene Wisuri.—1st ed.
     p. cm.
   ISBN 978-1-890434-80-9 (hardcover : alk. paper)
 1. United States—Race relations--Juvenile literature.
 2. Racism—Juvenile literature. I. Wisuri, Marlene, 1940- II. Title.

 E184.A1P37 2008
 305.800973—dc22

                                          2008000968
Printed in China

AFTON HISTORICAL SOCIETY PRESS
P.O. Box 100, Afton, MN 55001
800-436-8443
aftonpress@aftonpress.com
www.aftonpress.com

TO MY GRANDDAUGHTERS, Alex, Cyan, Baby Faith, and Sydney, knowing that the struggle for equality will continue with their generation, that they must fight racism and all forms of intolerance actively. That, like writer Nancy Butcher's hopes for her own children, "in the process of fighting they will lose sleep. That they will write angry letters denouncing intolerance to newspapers, government officials, corporations, and other institutions. That when they hear jokes or other remarks made at the expense of people of color, they will perform the awkward, separating act of speaking up. That they will not have to spend their lives smiling in order to get along. That they will develop steely glares, big mouths, some guts."

THOMAS PEACOCK

FOR RHIVERS, may you walk in freedom and light.

MARLENE WISURI

CONTENTS

foreword by Eric Jolly   8

preface   10

chapter 1:   we are all related   13

chapter 2:   who am i?   27

chapter 3:   racism throughout history   39

chapter 4:   unconscious and unintentional racism   55

chapter 5:   the missing stories   67

chapter 6:   in-your-face racism   77

chapter 7:   the best scouts in the cavalry   87

chapter 8:   to be free   99

appendix: "I Have a Dream" speech by Dr. Martin Luther King, Jr.   110

notes   112

selected bibliography   113

illustration credits   114

foreword

YOU HAVE JUST OPENED A GIFT. The book you are about to explore is full of gifts that will enrich your life and gifts that will help us grow together as a society.

These gifts come in the form of stories, the personal—often aching— stories of individuals' experiences of race and class in their everyday lives. It has been said that stories are like seeds, planted and nurtured by one generation to be harvested by the next, in a cycle that passes experience and wisdom to a future we will not see. Telling these stories is an act of faith: a faith in our common future, a faith that the best in our human nature will win out, and a faith that together we can touch the future.

The stories of this book are stories told with generosity and courage.

The framing of these stories is a call to the reader to join with the courageous and to become a part of transforming our world.

This book challenges us to accept a reality that is not perfect and to recognize the injustices, large and small, in the world around us. We must confront the discomforting truths to build a more comforting future. Clearly, the first step toward justice is the courageous recognition of injustice.

An elder once told me that he had spent some time thinking about that word "courage." He remarked that there may be many ways to define and demonstrate it. At its core, however, "Courage," he said, "is making a decision and taking responsibility for it."

I've often reflected on that conversation,

Opening your heart and mind is an amazing and liberating experience!

and, as is always the case, I am inclined to agree with my elders. On the battlefield, a courageous decision carries with it life and death responsibility. In social circumstances, an act of courage can mean isolation, discomfort, or even persecution. Courage may bring consequences that are difficult to bear, but courage also produces great satisfaction, joy, and an unending well of hope.

Embedded in this book's substance is a bold assertion that the future can and will be transformed by the courageous. Thomas Peacock's framing of these stories transforms individual experiences into universal lessons. In doing so he has created a powerful tool that will help us to better recognize injustice and take the next step towards building justice. I am hopeful that this book—this gift—may help us achieve one of our soul's deepest desires: **TO BE FREE**.

ERIC JOLLY, Ph.D.
PRESIDENT, SCIENCE MUSEUM OF MINNESOTA

PREFACE

IMAGINE IF WE WERE FREE of racism—free from the physical, emotional, psychological, and spiritual toll that it takes on both racists and those subjected to racism. IMAGINE TO BE FREE.

Often, however, just the mention of the word "racism" makes people nervous, like if the subject doesn't come up, maybe it will just go away completely. As if, maybe, it will slip forever into the recesses of a cave somewhere. Or maybe it will disappear magically, as if it never existed.

Many people of color, however, deal with the reality of racism in all its forms on a daily basis—in stores, in schools, at work, on the bus, while watching television, listening to music, browsing the Internet, or reading magazines and newspapers. They can't pretend it away because it is always there, in all its ugliness.

What if, however, we decided to acknowledge racism and talk about ways of preventing and alleviating it? And what if we began the discussion among young people, before they solidify their beliefs about people of other races? **TO BE FREE** was written to help facilitate this discussion.

The approach I have taken to the troubling issues of racism begins by acknowledging how closely all of humankind is related, and how over time we have come to emphasize our differences more than our commonalities. Each chapter in **TO BE FREE** asks pertinent questions about racism: What is meant by the idea of different "races" of human beings? What is racism and what are the different ways that racism manifests itself? What are the history and effects of racism in America? What is it like to be Asian American, black, white, Latino, or Native American? What is it like to be mixed race? When do we as individuals *decide* that we are white or black or Hmong or Dakota, or whatever race or ethnicity with which we identify? What kinds of things can young people, individuals, communities, and institutions (such as schools, governments, and places of worship) do to prevent and alleviate racism?

Each chapter ends with an activities section called "UNDERSTANDINGS," which provides questions for educators and students. Understanding is more than knowing facts about a topic. Understanding is getting the big picture, the big idea. Understanding is expressed by people in different ways. Learning activities can be designed to address the different facets of understanding: through explanation and interpretation; by revealing a historical or personal dimension to ideas and events, or telling meaningful stories; through application, using what we know in diverse and real contexts; through perspective, exposure to different points of view; through empathy, perceiving others' feelings, or trying on their perceptions; and through metacognition, cultivating self-knowledge, and reflecting on what we know and don't know.

It is my hope that readers of **TO BE FREE** will get the big idea about racism, and dare to imagine a society free of racism.

IMAGINE TO BE FREE!

Thomas Peacock

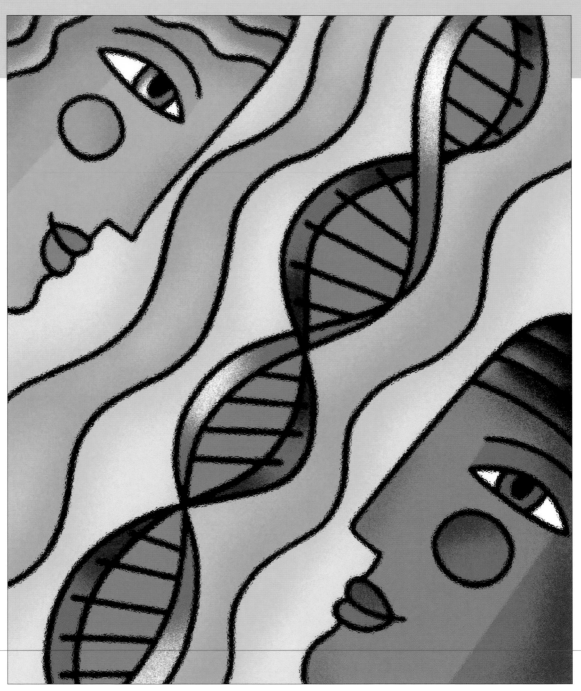

Our DNA makes each of us a unique individual.

chapter one

WE ARE ALL RELATED

EVERY PERSON who has ever lived is one of a kind. Each of us inherits physical characteristics from our biological parents, half from each. These characteristics are passed down from our parents to us through genes (biological units of heredity). Genes are made up of DNA (deoxyribonucleic acid), and it is our individual DNA that makes each and every one of us unique.

Genes determine the color of our skin and our hair, our height and the way our body looks. Skin color can be anywhere from very pale to very dark. Our hair comes in a variety of colors as well and ranges from short and spiral-shaped to long and straight. We are short and we are tall. We are thin and heavy. Our eyes or ears might be big or small, our noses broad or pointed, our lips thin or full.

Regardless of our many unique physical differences, however, we all share the same basic genetic materials. We are all one species (type of creature): human. We are all of one race: human.

what is race?

Perhaps in our need to make sense of the great diversity of humankind, we have given labels to the variety of our unique appearances. We have chosen to create "races" of humankind. But what is meant by the word "race"? One explanation often used is that the Earth has three or four races: Caucasian, Negroid, Mongoloid, and aboriginal Australian. That explanation, however, is too simple.

A museum exhibition, originally shown in France, titled "All of Us Are Related, Each of Us is Unique," has traveled across the United States to educate people about the remarkable diversity of humankind:

MAYBE I WAS in the second or third grade, but what I do remember clearly is this: I was walking home with a boy who lived down the road from me, figuring we'd stop to play at his place for a while. But when we got almost to his driveway he turned to me and said, 'You can't come any further. See, my dad, he don't like Injuns.'

Place and memory often meld into one.

Many years have passed. The boy, who knows what became of him. In my dreams he serves soft drinks at the reservation-owned casino and one of my aunties is his immediate supervisor. The house of his childhood, however, is still there, and the last time I was home I drove on by it. That's where he lived, I was thinking, the boy who I had thought was a friend.

The one whose father didn't like Injuns.

The diversity of human beings is so great and so complicated that it is impossible to classify the 5.5 billions of individuals into discrete "races". Some of our physical differences give the impression that it is possible to divide us into races. But when these physical characteristics are subjected to detailed study, it becomes clear that this is not possible. Instead, it becomes obvious that our physical diversity reflects continuous changes from one extreme to the other of the continents. To place any boundaries within this continuous diversity would be, therefore, completely arbitrary.[1]

There are, therefore, no "races," as we think of them. But this is not a new idea. Even as early as 1784, German philosopher and naturalist Johann von Herder concluded,

> The term race refers to a difference of origin which is non-existent for humans. . . . All physical types are inter-twined and follow hereditary characteristics . . . and in the end are only the shadows of a single large picture which extends through all the ages and over all the continents. [2]

Perhaps a better explanation of the concept of race is that it is a label given to a group of people that share different kinds of a temporary mix of genetic materials common to all humans. In fact, most anthropologists believe that all the different varieties of human beings on earth today share a common ancestor.

TO BE FREE

Anthropologist Ashley Montagu writes in his book *Man's Most Dangerous Myth* that science today supports this idea.

All humans belong to the same species and have the same remote ancestry. This is a conclusion to which all the relevant evidence of comparative anatomy, paleontology, serology, and genetics, points. On genetics grounds alone it is virtually impossible to conceive of the varieties of humankind as having originated separately as distinct lines from different ... ancestors.[3]

Race and adaptation

The relative isolation of our human ancestors within specific geographic regions contributed to the great physical diversity of humankind today. Living in family groups, small communities, and nation-states, the vast majority of the Earth's humans stayed in close proximity to the places of their birth throughout their lives. Imagine living your entire life within a few

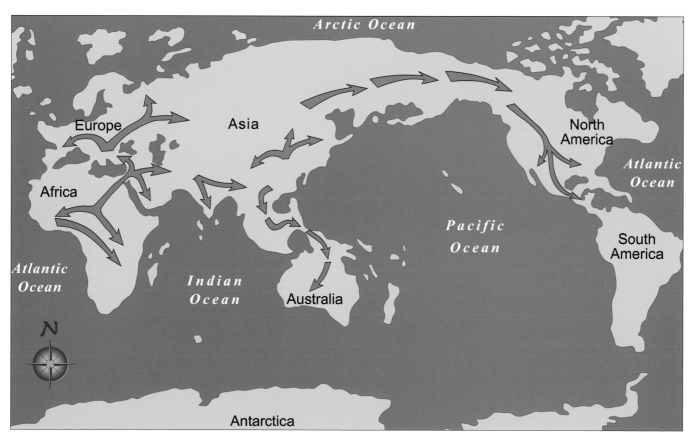

Humans migrated from Africa to all corners of the world.

miles of your hometown: that was the reality of most of our early ancestors.

Over time, people from certain regions who formed families began to acquire similar physical characteristics because they shared a common collection of traits, like skin color, facial features, hair type, and so on. As early humans migrated from Africa to all corners of the world—to Europe, Asia, Australia, and the Americas—they traveled from one geographic region to the next in search of food or safety. In these instances, different regional groups mingled, and their offspring inherited some of the combined physical traits of their parents.

Desert plants adapt to hot, dry conditions by developing thick skins.

As they migrated, early humans also had to adapt to their new surroundings. *Adaptation* is the process of physical or behavioral change to survive or better fit into a different environment. Adaptation is a biological event that takes place randomly and which is *evolutionary* (changes over time) in nature. One example of adaptation is the way desert plants developed thick skins to protect the water inside them from extremely hot climates. Bears have adapted to cold winters by developing thick coats of fur to keep them warm. Wolves found they were more successful hunters when they hunted together, and so adapted by forming packs while hunting.[4]

Adaptation is often used to explain how the different types of "races" can be identified by the climate in which they lived. Some body types and skin colors are better adapted to living in certain geographic areas, to living under different weather conditions. For example, people living in hot countries may have developed dark skin through a genetic adaptation that allowed their bodies to convert melanin, a pigment that darkens skin. Persons with this genetic trait were better adapted to deal with prolonged sunlight than people with light skin. People with dark skin are also less likely to be burned by the sun than those who are light-skinned, and they are less likely to get skin cancer. Likewise, people from the Arctic regions may have

TO BE FREE

that. Recent migrations prove this. For example, light-skinned people easily adapt to life in hot, sunny climates. Dark-skinned people easily adapt to cold, cloudy climates. Persons with fat-lidded eyes live all over the world.

Race Versus Ethnicity

For the most part, the racial categories we commonly use today actually better describe *ethnicity,* the combination of physical and cultural characteristics (such as languages, belief systems, and accepted ways of doing things) common to a group of people.

The term "white" is often used to describe people whose primary ancestry is out of northern Europe. "Black" is often used to describe people whose primary ancestry had origins in Africa. "Asian" combines distinctly different ethnic groups, including the peoples of India and all of Southeast Asia, Japan, Siberia, and China. "Native Americans" are referred to as those whose ancestors were the first settlers of North and South America.

Some body types and skin colors are better adapted to live in certain geographic areas.

developed thick, squat bodies through adaptations that allowed them to retain more body heat in a very cold climate. People with fat-lidded eyes may be better protected against the glare of the sun.

But human beings are even more adaptable than

We may never know what "race" our early ancestors belonged to, and whether their skin color was black, or brown, or white. But does it matter? Each was a uniquely beautiful member of the same species: human. Despite our different cultures and different languages, we are all related.

A "colored-only" drinking fountain on the county courthouse lawn, Halifax, North Carolina, April, 1938.

TO BE FREE

So how did we get to this place along the road of human existence where racism has become the troubling issue that it is? It is a place where many Americans are excluded from sharing the great bounty of our country because of the color of their skin. It is a place where a civil war was fought, in large part, over the enslavement of blacks. And it is a place where whole tribal nations were exterminated simply because they were Native peoples. How did we get here?

δετεrmιπιπg ςuperιorιτy

Ethnocentrism, the belief that one's own ethnic group is superior to all others, has probably existed for many thousands of years, and is common in most cultures. The early Egyptians believed that non-Egyptians were less human. Only by moving to Egypt and acquiring language, culture, and citizenship could non-Egyptians be considered truly human. Ancient Greece relied on slaves, who were also considered less human than citizens of Greece. However, the slaves were a variety of colors and sizes and cultures, so the Greeks' beliefs in superiority were not based on race. Instead, to the people of ancient Greece, Greeks were superior humans. The rest of the people of the world were barbarians.

And so people have a tendency to believe their own culture is better than others. One can imagine all the things that have been said through the years that helped confirm these beliefs: Those people look funny. They dress really different. Some of them don't wear many clothes. They talk like FROGS. They believe trees have souls. I hear they even eat dogs. Who would think that? Isn't that just crazy?

Throughout history these beliefs have been used to persecute others because of their religious beliefs, culture, or social behavior.

Europeans were the first to base human superiority on race alone. European exploration of the wider world brought with it a new awareness of human diversity, indeed of the great diversity of life on Earth in all its forms. Explorers brought back to Europe plants of all varieties and animals of all shapes and colors and sizes, many of which were unknown in Europe. They also returned with stories of other people different from themselves. In some instances they brought these very people back to Europe.

European religious beliefs held that humans originated from one woman and one man—the Biblical Adam and Eve. And so, for many Europeans, learning about people so different from themselves challenged long-held beliefs about the common origins of humans. To Europeans, the Africans, Asians, and Native Americans, the explorers had encountered certainly *looked* different from the mental picture they had of that first human pair.

From the European perspective, the first humans had always been depicted as white people. Dark skin was considered ugly and characteristic of people with less morality, less intelligence. Dark people were seen as primitive, less "civilized."

The Europeans also clung to a belief that humans represented the highest life forms on earth, and that the more animals were like humans (in appearance or behavior), the more perfect they were. Animals were graded based on how similar they were to humans, with humans at the top of the order. Animals that differed greatly from humans were placed at the bottom of the scale. Animals that shared some behavior traits with humans ended up closer to the top.

Confronted with new knowledge of great diversity in mankind, certain Europeans decided to order human beings the same way animals had been ordered, except instead of human beings at the top of the order, Europeans put themselves there. They placed Asians, Africans, Native Americans, and other groups below them.

An early engraving of racial types.

TO BE FREE

The belief that Europeans were at the top of some order of human beings, and that all other people were below them (and thus less human) was one that was held in the scientific community as well. This idea suggested that Europeans were thousands of years more advanced than other people. Of course this view reflected European *biases* (prejudices).

Despite the common European belief in European superiority, scientists did not agree on the number of different human races. The table below, from author Stephen Molnar, shows how four of Europe's most well-known eighteenth-century scientists classified human beings into races.[5]

One American scientist, Samuel Morton, collected thousands of Native American skulls for his studies. He compared these skulls to the European skulls in his collection and found the European skulls had a larger brain capacity than the Native skulls, thus indicating to him that Europeans were superior in intelligence and character. These conclusions have since been discredited by modern science.

While early scientists believed that humans were certainly much more highly developed than apes or monkeys, what really separated them (according to their beliefs) was that only humans possessed souls. Early on, many Europeans (as well as their American counterparts) struggled to determine whether

CARL LINNAEUS (1735)	GEORGES BUFFON (1749)	JOHANN FRIEDRICH BLUMENBACH (1781)	GEORGES CUVIER (1790)
American (Reddish)	Laplander	Caucasoid	Caucasoid
European (White)	Tartar	Mongoloid	Mongoloid
Asiatic (Yellow)	South Asiatic	American Indian	Negroid
Negro (Black)	European	Ethiopian	
	Ethiopian	Malay	
	American	American	

One way that early scientists sought to prove the superiority of Europeans was through the study of brain size and shape. The larger the brain capacity of the skull, it was believed, the greater the intelligence and character of the individual. Broad, elongated skulls were associated with "lower" humans.

blacks and Native people were fully human and whether they possessed souls. People with dark skin were considered accursed, that their fate was to serve a master, the white people. After slavery became established in the United States, and many American blacks became Christians, this question needed to be settled, particularly because of the issue of slavery. As a result, the prevailing belief became one that suggested blacks were a different category of human, one whose fate, determined by the Creator, was to be enslaved. As Paul Harvey wrote in a piece called "A Servant of Servants Shall He Be,"

One popular argument was that people were indeed created by God to stay in varying degrees of freedom or subjection [slavery], and that for some to enjoy full liberty, others would have to be servants; this best served the happiness of the whole.[6]

These *faulty* (incorrect, defective) arguments were eventually used to justify slavery and the mass removal and genocide of Native people in the Americas.

PREJUDICE OR RACISM?

The terms used to describe feelings of superiority among humans can be confusing. We have learned that ethnocentrism, the belief that one ethnic group or culture is superior to another, has probably existed for many thousands of years and is common in most cultures.

Prejudice, on the other hand, happens when we form an opinion or make a judgment about others based on stereotypes, distortions, or omissions. For example, early during the second Gulf War, some Americans expressed their prejudice against the French people because the government of France opposed the American invasion of Iraq. In some American business establishments, French fries were renamed "Freedom Fries." This was prejudice. Not all French people opposed American involvement in the war.

An early poster denouncing slavery, c.1887.

TO BE FREE

So what, then, is racism? *Racism* is founded on the belief that physical and behavioral diversity in humans is determined by their genetic makeup, and that these differences can be ranked on a scale from higher ability and potential to lower ability and potential. Anthropologist Ashley Montagu explains it this way:

> Three criteria are involved in the racist view: (1) physical traits, (2) mental capacities and abilities, and (3) the ability to achieve a high level of civilization. To put it briefly, the racist believes that physical characteristics, capacity, and creativity are genetically related, fixed and unchangeable. He may never have formulated his belief in these words but in his own mind, however, vaguely this is what it amounted to.[7]

Racist beliefs *manifest* (show) themselves in different ways, each of which is covered in a chapter in this book. Some of those ways include:

UNINTENTIONAL RACISM: This is unconscious racism. For example, why do some white women clutch their purses when minority teenagers draw near? Why do some white men hesitate when getting into an elevator full of black men? Why do so many whites have involuntary negative reactions when flashed *subliminal* (shown momentarily, hidden) images of black faces in social experiments? This is the kind of racism known as "white privilege."

INSTITUTIONAL RACISM: This is racism in institutions such as schools and governments. Other examples include what society considers acceptable art or music, and in the recording and telling of history (whose perspective of history).

OVERT, IN-YOUR-FACE RACISM: This is racism that is raw, angry, *overt* (obvious), and uncompromising. "I hate blacks! I hate Asians! I hate whites!"

INTERNALIZED RACISM: People who have been *oppressed* (been the targets of racism) sometimes develop a twisted form of self-hate because of their race. History is full of examples of *internalized* (to take into one's way of thinking) racism. Some of the best scouts in the U.S. Cavalry used against Native people were fellow Natives.

ᖴᑌᒪᒪ ᑕᏆᖇᑕᒪᕦ

Despite the human tendency to focus on differences, we humans share much in common. We come in all sizes, from the Pygmies in Africa and

We are all related.

In this life we prepare for things, for moments and events and situations. . . . We worry about wrongs, think about injustices, read what Tolstoy and Ruskin has to say. . . . Then, all of a sudden, the issue is not whether we agree with what we have heard and read and studied. . . . The issue is us, and what we have become.

—ROBERT COLES

Oceania (islands of the Pacific), who average four-and-a-half feet tall, to the Nilotic people of East Africa, who average six-and-a-half feet tall. We come in all colors, from very pale (as with many people from Northern Europe) to very dark (as with many people from the Congo in Africa or New Guinea). We speak many languages and have unique ways of being. Our physical diversity resulted from the relative isolation and geography of our ancestors as well as from our unique genetic inheritance.

"Race" is a cultural term that has been used to describe the great diversity of humankind. Biologically speaking, however, we are all one species: human. We are all one race: human.

TO BE FREE

THEMES

☞ **All humankind** is related, one species, and one race—the human race.

☞ **"Ethnicity,"** a combination of physical and cultural characteristics that explains the great diversity of humankind.

☞ **Groups** often feel their own group is superior to other groups in one way or another.

☞ **Modern racism** has its roots in Europe.

☞ **Racism** is expressed in many ways.

ACTIVITIES TO PROMOTE UNDERSTANDING

1. Do a library or a Web search on the Ice Ages or global warming. What kinds of physical changes might humans make to adapt to the new conditions? Cultural changes? Write or tell a story about what life would be like under these conditions.

2. Interview a family member about your ethnicity, the combination of physical and cultural characteristics, including languages, beliefs, ways of being and doing that make up your background. Some questions to ask include: What are my family's countries of origins? How might my physical characteristics be a result of my ancestor's origins? What cultural characteristics have been passed down from generation to generation in my family?

3. Think of things you can do that you feel you can do better than most others. For example, maybe you're a star athlete. Or maybe you easily "get" math and this is reflected in A grades. Think about things you feel your school does better than other schools. Maybe it's newer or bigger or friendlier or has a winning basketball team. Make a list of these things about yourself or your school. In what ways is this sense of personal or group superiority similar to ethnocentrism? In what ways is it different? Is the need to feel superior natural or is it learned?

4. Choose an ethnic minority that was targeted for racism by seventeenth- to nineteenth-century Europeans: blacks, Native Americans, or Asians. Use resources in the library or on the Web to help explain how the racism directed toward the group manifested itself. How was racism directed against the group expressed similarly to or differently than the racism directed against other groups? What common threads of racism link all the groups?

5. Imagine you are a different ethnicity. Now, imagine you are the only one of your ethnicity in a large crowd—the only white person, the only black, the only female, the only male. What kinds of *apprehension* (uneasiness, nervousness, concern) might the crowd be feeling? What kinds of apprehension might you be feeling? Where do these concerns come from, and what can we do to reduce or eliminate them?

Children collecting berries at Nett Lake.

who am i?

WE KNOW that we are one species (human), and that there is but one race, the human race. However, when we describe the physical and cultural differences among humans, we still use the word "race" when we are actually describing an ethnic group. An ethnic group has its own cultural and physical characteristics. In this chapter, however, we will use the term "racial identity" because it is commonly used to describe the ways in which ethnic groups identify their own uniqueness.

How is it that we come to identify with a "race" or "races"—our racial self-identity?

"I'm black."

"I'm Asian."

"I'm white."

"I'm Latino."

"I'm Native American."

"My dad is black and my mom is white. I suppose I'm both, but as far as I'm concerned, I'm black."

When do we, as individuals, make these determinations, and what is the basis for them?

We begin making decisions about who we are early in life. Even as infants, we begin to evaluate ourselves. Through interaction we begin to notice physical differences between ourselves and others. We also begin to form opinions about others. In what ways are others like me? How are they different from me?

By three to seven years of age, we are well on the way to forming our identities and determining our personal values in terms of our racial self-identities. These two things—who we are and the value we place on who we are—form the basis of racial self-identity.

I WAS A LITTLE KID, and the playground at my school was a big, scary place. And it seemed that at every recess, a group of town boys would tease a Native girl who rode the reservation bus with the rest of us "Injuns," as they called us, into school each day. Their words were sharp as knives, incessant. "Hey, squaw! You gonnum scalp us?" She would plead with them to stop, but they would continue their taunting until she cried uncontrollably and chased them all over the playground. Ultimately, she would tire and then cower in a corner like a wounded fawn, and her tormenters would encircle her like jackals and kill her spirit with the sharp spears of their tongues. Only once do I remember she caught one of them and beat him. When I saw this, the inside me, the part that never showed, rose and gave her a standing ovation.

Most of the time, however, she would suffer the poison of their words. I remember as I watched and listened to the daily, awful scene, my stomach muscles would tighten and sometimes I would almost bend over in pain. I wanted to say some-thing to them, to yell at them, beg of them. "Leave her alone. Please leave her alone, she has done nothing to you."

But I never said a word. I was stopped cold by fear. Fear that they would turn on me, that I would become their target.

So the years passed, and the unrelenting torment continued. And then one day, in the sixth or seventh grade, the girl just quit coming to school. Me, I grew in stature and confidence, and became good with my fists.

I was not teased.

Some years ago I was reading the home-town newspaper and noticed her name in the obituary column. She died young. I don't know the circumstances. Her for-mer tormenters are now the city fa-thers—city councilmen, business owners, bankers, and teachers all. I am hopeful they have learned from the folly of their past.

I know I have.

MAKING DECISIONS ABOUT WHO WE ARE

We all have multiple identities, not just our racial identities. These identities are based on many things, including our family, where we live, our physical characteristics, beliefs, and what others think of us. We are "Isaiah's daughter," "Amos's son," "Amy's sister." Some of our identities are based on our spiritual beliefs. Other identities are based on where we live. We are Wisconsinites, Minnesotans, Duluthians, or Red Lakers. And still other identities are based on age. We are youngsters, teens, adults, or seniors. We are many things, and we contain many identities, all wrapped up in a single individual.

How do you identify yourself? Try this simple exercise: take a piece of paper and write on the top, "I am (your name) _____." Next, write down all the things you can think of that define you. Such as your interests, beliefs, hobbies, talents (math aptitude, musical abilities, athletically inclined, etc.) and aspirations. How many did you come up with? How do you describe yourself?

After you have looked at your list, ask yourself what you forgot. Write these things down as well. Now, look at the completed list. All of the ways you've described yourself make up your *identity*.

Learning about racial issues through an exhibit at the Science Museum of Minnesota in Saint Paul.

It's interesting when we compare the lists of people from different ethnic backgrounds. White teens don't often mention they are white, but blacks or Asians or Latinos or Native youth (sometimes as a group referred to as "people of color") who have a strong racial identity will often include on their lists "black," "Dakota," "Hmong," or whatever they consider to be their racial identity. Why is that the case? The simple answer is that they include their racial identity because they are probably often described by others as being black, Asian, Latino, or Native.

So, decisions about our identity are strongly influenced by our experiences with others. What do our parents or grandparents say we are? What do our friends say about who we are? What do our classmates say? And what do others with whom we interact every day say about who we are, either by their words or their actions? Teachers, the principal, people at the checkout counter at the grocery store—anyone we meet and interact with may give us a sense of who we are by the words they use, and sometimes just by the way they act around us. Even when we turn on the television we are told who we are. Hmong are *this*. Being black is *this*. Being Native is *this*. Whites are *this*.

As a result, we see and hear and *intuit* (feel or sense) a lot of information about who we are, and our minds begin to form an image of what it is to

be Native or what it means to be Latino, and so on, and eventually we take in all of this information and use it to form our definitions of ourselves.

> I'M WHITE.
> I'M HMONG.
> AND I'M WHITE BECAUSE . . .
> OR I'M HMONG BECAUSE . . .

We begin to notice the physical features (particularly skin color, hair type, and facial features) of others and ourselves at a young age—especially skin color. As we get older (six or seven years old or older) we begin to notice that "black" is actually not black, but many shades of different browns, from dark to light brown. We also notice that "white" isn't really white at all, that it is many shades, from light to tan.

As we enter adolescence, the physical differences we notice in people become more important to our developing sense of racial identity. All teens begin asking the same question of themselves: Who am I? However, young people of color take this question a step further and ask: What does it mean to be Ojibwe? Dakota? Hmong? Black? Korean? Who am I racially?

Why do they ask this? *Because this is how others see them.* Often, when white adults see a teen

TO BE FREE

who happens to be black, they think, "black teenager." Many times, when a teacher, regardless of his or her own racial identity, sees a group of Native teens, they think, "Native kids."

Psychologist Dr. William Cross has described how many black youth develop their racial identity.[8] His description can be applied to other teens of color, including Native, Latino, and Asian youths. At an early age, Dr. Cross has said, people of color begin to notice that the *dominant* (main or most valued) traits of what is considered "American" come from white culture. Seeing this, they decide that, in America, it is probably better to be white. They begin to absorb the stereotypes about people from their specific ethnic backgrounds, more negative than positive. It is at this point when it is crucial for parents and teachers to affirm to teens of color all the positive things about being black, Asian, Latino, or Native.

Then, the young person has his or her first personal experiences with racism. Maybe she is called a racially derogative name. Or maybe he notices that some white adults get nervous when they see him coming. Or maybe her white friends begin dating and she notices that she isn't being asked out by any white boys. These two early events—realizing American culture often values white traits and experiencing racism firsthand—influence young people as they develop their own understanding of what it means, for them, to be black, Latino, Asian, or Native, or any other ethnicity.

For most white teens, racial identity develops in a different way from that of people of color. Whites don't generally think about being white. Psychologist and Spelman University President Dr. Beverly Daniel Tatum writes in her book *Why Are All the Black Kids Sitting Together in the Cafeteria?* that the white students she teaches are often at a loss when asked to describe their ethnicity.

> I often begin the classes and workshops I lead by asking participants to reflect on their own social class and ethnic background in small discussion groups. The first question I pose is one that most people of color answer without hesitation: What is your class and ethnic background?" White participants, however, often pause before responding. On one such occasion a young white woman quickly described herself as middle-class but seemed stumped as to how to describe herself ethnically. Finally, she said, "I'm just normal!" What did she mean? She explained that she did not identify with any particular ethnic heritage, and that she was a lot like the other people who lived in her very homogenous, white middle-class community. But her choice of words was

telling. If she is "just normal", are those who are different from her "just abnormal"?

Why did Dr. Tatum's student use the word "normal" to describe herself? She used this word because being white is the *norm* (standard or typical)—the majority of Americans are white. Young people of color need to develop a racial identity that is positive by not believing the negative stereotypes of people of their ethnic background, and by accepting and embracing all the positive things about their ethnicity. Whites also need to develop a positive racial identity, one that doesn't accept the idea of white superiority that *pervades* (is everywhere) our society.

The value of who we are

Identity becomes even more complicated in American culture because our society has historically placed more value on certain traits, making other traits less desirable. Whiteness (being white) has historically carried with it certain privileges. Early in American history, for example, only white male landowners could vote. Most white plantation owners owned black slaves. White politicians denied American citizenship to Native Americans until the early twentieth century. Even today, being white has certain privileges. In general, whites have a higher standard of living, better jobs, better education, and they have the privilege of seeing a preponderance of other whites in important positions of power. But perhaps the greatest privilege of being white is the privilege of not having to think about being white.

There are traits beyond ethnicity that are valued in our society. A thin body is valued in American society. One that is fat is not. Young people who are overweight are often teased for being heavy. "You should lose some weight," someone might say to them. Thinness is particularly valued in girls. In general, thin, attractive girls are treated more favorably by both males and females in American society.

Males have traditionally been more highly valued individuals in our society than females. One example of this is that males with the same level of education as their female counterparts earn a higher average income. They are also paid more for doing the same job; on average, women make only 75.5 cents for every dollar that men earn. Males are also found in more positions of power, as mayors and council members, legislators and congressional representatives, as members of the presidential cabinet, and as vice president and president.

Another highly-valued trait in American culture is youth. The mass media (television, radio, newspapers, Internet) target young audiences. It is important, they tell us, to feel young, to be young, and to look young. Clothing fashions cater to the

TO BE FREE

young. Music targets a young audience. Wrinkle creams, hair dye to hide the gray, surgical procedures to remove sagging skin, and other beauty and cosmetic treatments are pushed on older people so they may look younger.

In American culture, Christianity is often more highly valued than other religions. American Indians who chose not to become Christians were not given the freedom to practice their own religion until the 1978 American Indian Religious Freedom Act. After the events of September 11, 2001, some people of the Muslim faith were openly discriminated against by fellow Americans.

Wealth is another important and elevated trait in America: poor people are not as valued as those in the middle and upper classes. Proof of this is even found in American slang: "Man, that's really ghetto" is a phrase used to describe something unworthy or shabby. And more and more, homeless people have become the targets of violent attacks in some cities.

All of these traits, and others—along with the values placed on them by American society—contribute to our understanding of ourselves.

Mixed Identity

Author Barbara Cruz wrote in her book *Multiethnic*

American advertising has marketed the virtues of being young, thin, and white.

Teens and Cultural Identity about a young girl who came from a multiracial background:

> Fourteen-year-old Mahin Root was looking forward to enrolling at Page High School in Greensboro, North Carolina. As she filled out the school registration form, she left blank the question that asked about her race. Since Mahin's father is white and her mother is black, she felt she could not choose just one category, either "black" or "white."[9]

The number of interracial marriages in the United States has doubled since 1967.

Situations like the one experienced by Mahin often occur for those of us who are "mixed," or who identify with more than one racial group. In reality, of course, all humans are "mixed." For example, individual black people and individual white people may be more closely related genetically in certain instances than individual black people may be to other black people, or individual white people to other white people. Being "mixed" really means just being human.

But it wasn't until 1967 that the U.S. Supreme Court declared that laws that prohibited interracial marriages were unconstitutional. Since then, the number of interracial marriages has more than doubled, resulting in many more children who self-identify with more than one racial group.

Much of the early concern about the children of interracial marriages was based on racism—the idea that people of color were inferior to whites. There were other concerns, however. What would these children be called? Black? White? Half-breeds? (The term "half-breed" was once commonly used to describe people of mixed white and Native heritage. Today, it is considered offensive to use the term.) Would they be treated poorly by all ethnic groups because of their mixed heritage? Would their self-identity suffer from an inability to identify with one or more of their ethnic backgrounds? How would other children treat them? How would this treatment affect them in school and the community?

Until recently, the children of black-white marriages were always considered black by most people in society. In fact, persons with any trace of black heritage were considered black. Today, they are more often identified by others as mixed race, or mixed. Mixed children who are adopted by parents of one ethnic heritage often more closely identify with their adoptive parents' heritage, probably because their own ethnic heritage is *deemphasized* (played down). For example, adoptive white parents may know little about what it means to be black or Native, and may not be able or willing to offer anything of use regarding that background to the child. At other times, the adoptive parents simply deemphasize racial identity altogether and the child does the same.

Some young people from mixed backgrounds have poor self-image because they are confused or have negative feelings about their racial identities. Am I black? Am I white? Am I Native? Am I Hmong? Physically, they may look white, yet feel Native on the inside. Physically, they may look black, yet identify with their Latino heritage. They may look Hmong, yet know nothing about Hmong culture because they are not being raised in Hmong culture. And sometimes they have difficulty *expressing* (talking about or recognizing) their feelings about this. As a result, their confusion may manifest itself in poor grades, an inability to concentrate, behavior problems, or feelings of loneliness.

There are ways to help young people who are mixed to develop positive racial identities. Professors of social work Ruth G. McRoy and Edith M. Freeman suggest the following:

PARENTS should talk freely about the young person's racial heritage and encourage young people to discuss it with others.

PARENTS need to acknowledge that their own racial background is different from their children and encourage the child's mixed identity.

YOUNG PEOPLE need to be encouraged to develop friendships with people of all colors and backgrounds.

ADULTS need to give "mixed" children opportunities to have positive interactions and role models with people of all colors and backgrounds.

ADULTS need to model non-stereotyped attitudes toward people of other racial backgrounds.

FAMILIES need to encourage a sense that being "mixed" is good.[10]

When young people enter adolescence, the acceptance of their *peers* (friends and fellow teens) often becomes more important than the acceptance of their parents. Teens who are mixed may feel rejected by whites because of their mixed heritage or feel rejected by blacks or Natives or Latinos or members of whatever ethnicities make up their background because they are "mixed breeds."

Megan, a student of mixed white and Ojibwe heritage, talked about some of her experiences in the book *The Seventh Generation: Native Students Speak About Finding the Good Path:*

> I'm really light complected, so sometimes I feel like I belong in both worlds. Like, if I said I went to a pow-wow with my cousin, I'd feel

kind of self-conscious. I know inside I belong there, but people are looking at me, walking around saying things like, "Who's that White girl wannabe at our pow-wow?" And I know they're thinking that, and I understand why they think that. But it's kind of hard because I know I'm not [a wannabe]. I mean like all my brothers are dark. I kind of joke around sometimes with Tom [brother] that I'm the white sheep of the family instead of the black sheep. Sometimes, I do feel like a wannabe because my skin is so light, but I consider myself an Indian. If anybody has ever said anything racist, I don't think I've really felt intimidated because I stand up to them.[11]

There are many well-known people of mixed backgrounds. Tiger Woods describes himself as "one-eighth Caucasian, one-quarter black, one-eighth American Indian, one-quarter Thai, and one-quarter Chinese."[12] Early in his golfing career, reporters often wrote about him as a "black" golfer, but Woods would correct them, saying he was proud of his mixed heritage. "It's just who I am," he said.

Singer Mariah Carey has always been proud of her mixed background. Her mother is Irish and white and her father is Venezuelan and black. She knows from experience, though, that some people are not accepting of mixed marriages. Her family suffered through some terrible situations because of this hatred: their dogs were poisoned, their belongings were vandalized, and Carey and her siblings were taunted. "The thing about me is I always felt like an outsider," Carey has said. "That's partly because I'm multiracial."[13]

Actress Halle Berry, whose father is black and mother is white, had some difficulty while growing up because of her mixed background. She recalls being called "zebra" by both black and white children. She credits her mother for giving her a strong sense of self-worth and pride, knowing that what is important is on the inside. She proudly identifies with her black heritage.

Barack Obama with his white, maternal grandparents, Stanley and Madelyn Dunham, in the 1970s.

TO BE FREE

proudly valuing who you are

Who are we? We are Isaiah's daughter, Amos's son, Amy's sister. We are Buddhists, Christians, Catholics, Lutherans, Muslims, and Jews. We are Wisconsinites, Minnesotans, Duluthians, and Red Lakers. We are children, teens, adults, and seniors. We are boys, girls, men, women, Democrats, Republicans, liberals, and conservatives. And we are black, white, Asian, Latino, Native, and more. We have our own ways, our unique physical characteristics, languages, and beliefs.

We are one species, human. We are one race, human. We are some and all of these things, proudly wrapped up in a single individual.

EACH OF US IS UNIQUE.

CHAPTER UNDERSTANDINGS

THEMES

☞ **Each of us** has multiple identities, including racial identity, that make up who we are.

☞ **Racial identity** is strongly influenced by our experiences with others.

☞ **Society** places more or less value on certain things, including people's racial background.

☞ **People** with mixed racial backgrounds sometimes confront issues those with a single racial identity do not.

ACTIVITIES TO PROMOTE UNDERSTANDING

1. Do the exercise "Who am I" on page 29. Give each item you list a value (highly valued, valued, not valued) as you see it. Then, put stars next to the three things you value most about yourself. Share the list with your peers.

2. Do a library or Web search for life information (childhood, family, career, etc.) about actress Halle Berry, singer Mariah Carey, or golfer Tiger Woods. Then, develop a list of the things that may make up the identity of the person you've chosen, including his or her racial identity. What things do you think they value highly in themselves? Are there any things that you think they might not value? Why?

3. Working with a partner, take the role of a parent or young person while your partner takes the role you haven't chosen. Using the techniques social workers Ruth G. McRoy and Edith M. Freeman developed to help young people who are mixed cultivate positive racial identities, develop a dialogue between a mixed-race young person and a parent.

Christopher Columbus among Native people.

chapter three

RACISM THROUGHOUT HISTORY

THIS CHAPTER deals with only a small slice of the story about racism that has existed throughout the history of America. Reading about racism makes most of us uncomfortable. The stories tug at us emotionally. It can be difficult to read about racism, but knowing the story is necessary.

Some white people might feel angry when they read about the history of racism; they might feel that they are being forced to *atone for* (answer for or apologize for) the sins of the past, for the acts other whites committed against Native people, Asian Americans, or blacks. They might cry out in their anger, "We accept what happened to Native people. We accept what happened to blacks and Asian Americans as well. But we are innocent. We have done nothing wrong."

And they are right. They are innocent.

The horrendous acts committed against people of color throughout history were committed by other people from other generations. On other occasions, however, whites may feel guilt instead of anger. They may feel guilt because of what happened in the past. This guilt is unfounded. We need to ask ourselves, "Guilt for what?" They have nothing to feel personally guilty about.

But anger and guilt are normal emotions. We need to feel these emotions sometimes in order to grow and move on.

People of color often feel a whole range of emotions when reading about historical racism directed against their ancestors: anger, grief, or determination to not allow it to happen to them. These feelings are also normal. We need to feel these emotions as well to grow and move on.

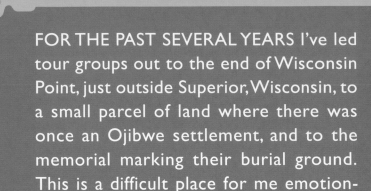

FOR THE PAST SEVERAL YEARS I've led tour groups out to the end of Wisconsin Point, just outside Superior, Wisconsin, to a small parcel of land where there was once an Ojibwe settlement, and to the memorial marking their burial ground. This is a difficult place for me emotionally. My voice almost always breaks as I tell groups, Native and non-Native alike, how my ancestors were moved against their will from this beautiful and sacred place, that even their graves were scooped up and moved to the edge of a cemetery several miles away. You see, for so many Native people, history is not simply some distant telling of events we read about in books or see in videos. History is something real and now. History sings to me each time I stand in that sacred place, and the song is our Native story, passed down from generation to generation. History flows from the spirits of my ancestors through me and goes down into my heart, and it comes out in words through my fingers and finds its way onto the pages of books.

What good is it, then, to bring up what happened in the past? Wouldn't it just be easier to let the past be forgotten and to move on? No, because that would allow us to deny what occurred in the past. Denial is not healthy because it is an attempt to put things neatly away into closets and leave them there. These are stories that we need to confront in order that all of us might heal and move on.

History is also a great teacher; history can help explain why we are where we are today. And perhaps most important, knowing our history might teach us to not walk down that road again, to avoid the mistakes those before us committed, and, using our past, to grow beyond our history.

The history many of us have been taught is only part of the story, and its tellings have *withheld* (to hold back or hide) other truths. The stories you'll read in this chapter are some of those other truths. Together, these truths will begin to form a more complete picture of what really happened.

THE GENOCIDE OF NATIVE PEOPLE

The first voyage of Christopher Columbus to the Americas in 1492 marked the beginning of the *genocide* (the mass killing or eradication of an entire people because of their ethnicity or religious beliefs) of Native people. The West Indies were populated by the Arawak people, who greeted Columbus's ships when they arrived. The Spaniards enslaved

TO BE FREE

the Arawaks, forcing them to mine for gold. Many of those who were enslaved died in the mines. Others died from illnesses and starvation. Those who refused to become slaves were killed by the explorers' muskets or swords. Many committed suicide rather than face becoming a slave. The population of the Native people plummeted. The Native population of Haiti, for example, went from 250,000 to zero between 1492 and 1650.[14] Across the Caribbean, millions of people died.

Protestors at a replica of Columbus's ship, "Nina", during its visit to Duluth, summer 2007.

Historian Howard Zinn writes that Las Casas, the man who transcribed Columbus's journal, documents the *demise* (extinction) of the Native population.

> When he arrived in Hispaniola in 1508, Las Casas says, "There were 60,000 people living on this island, including the Indians; so that from 1494 to 1508, over three million people had perished from war, slavery, and the mines. Who in future generations will believe this? I myself writing it as a knowledgeable eyewitness can hardly believe it."[15]

Columbus acknowledged in his own journal, and in the journals written by the Jesuits (a religious order of Catholic missionaries) who accompanied him, the slaughter of millions of innocent people. Therein lies a lesson of history. What is taught as history is usually written by the victors, and is not necessarily the whole story, or even the truth.

As other explorers and European settlers arrived in the Americas, the Native population began a rapid decline because of the introduction of diseases such as measles, smallpox, and mumps, against which they had no *immunity* (safety against a particular disease), as well as war, starvation, suicide, and, sometimes, *wanton* (without reason and cruel) mass killings. The Spanish explorers led by

Hernán Cortes slaughtered the Aztecs of Mexico and Central America by the thousands. Francisco Pizarro did the same to the Incas of South America. The Native populations near the first English settlement in Virginia, as well the Narragansett, Wampanoag, and Pequot tribes of Massachusetts, lost thousands from diseases and warfare with the arrival of the new settlers.

How many died? We may never know the answer, but we can be sure it was in the millions. Perhaps ten million in North America alone, and likely more, were annihilated between 1492 and the beginning of the twentieth century. Why did this happen? Howard Zinn sums it up this way:

> Behind the English invasion of North America, behind their massacre of Indians, their deception, their brutality, was that special powerful drive born in civilizations based on private property. It was amorally ambiguous drive; the need for space, for land, was a real human need. But in conditions of scarcity, in a barbarous epoch of history ruled by competition, this human need was transformed into the murder of whole peoples.[16]

Slavery

Until they learned and perfected the ability to grow corn, a skill taught to them by the local

TO BE FREE

Natives, many of the earliest European settlers of Virginia starved; their numbers were reduced from more than five hundred to just sixty during the winter of 1609–1610. But with corn, they could eat and live. Soon, they also learned to grow tobacco, which would become their chief export crop. Growing tobacco required a lot of land and was labor intensive. The Native population refused to tend the settlers' fields and could not be forced to do so because the English newcomers were outnumbered by their Native neighbors.

By 1619, African slaves, a million or more, had already been kidnapped and brought across the ocean to work the Spanish and Portuguese plantations of the Caribbean and South America. For the English settlers of the American colonies, too,

African American men, women, and children being auctioned off in front of a crowd of men, 1861.

In 1862, President Abraham Lincoln decreed in the Emancipation Proclamation that on January 1, 1863, "all persons held as slaves shall forever be free."

the answer to their need for labor was the slave trade. Tobacco, and later cotton, would become the main agricultural exports of the new nation, and both crops required labor.

The first slave ship arrived in Marblehead, Massachusetts, in 1637. By 1800, between ten and fifteen million Africans had been forced into slavery and brought to the Americas against their wills.[17] It is estimated that, in all, fifty million Africans were lost to slavery. By 1860, there were four million slaves living in America. The conditions in which they were brought to this country were appalling. Just surviving the journey to America was difficult. Historian Howard Zinn describes the horrific conditions:

> The marches to the coast, sometimes for 1,000 miles, with people shackled around the neck, under whip and gun, were death marches, in which two of every five blacks died. On the coast, they were kept in cages until they were picked and sold. . . . Then they were packed aboard slave ships, in spaces not much bigger than coffins, chained together in the dark, wet slime of the ship's bottom, choking in the stench of their own excrement. . . . Under these conditions, perhaps one in every three blacks transported overseas died, but the huge profits made it

TO BE FREE

worthwhile for the slave trader, and so the blacks were packed into the holds like fish.[18]

Keeping such large numbers of slaves in line was accomplished through the use of both physical force and psychological means. Whipping, mutilation, hanging, and burning were common. Some of the forms of psychological cruelty slaveowners used against their slaves included separating families—fathers and mothers, sisters and brothers—and creating tension between lowly "field slaves," who worked the fields, and "house slaves," who tended to matters within the white slaveowner's home.

It would not be until the country lapsed into a civil war, sparked by, among other reasons, the question of slavery, that the institution was abolished. In 1862, President Abraham Lincoln issued the Emancipation Proclamation, which stated that on the first day of January 1863, "all persons held as slaves shall forever be free."

The Civil War would go on to claim more than 600,000 lives on both sides. After victory by the North, Congress enacted the 13th amendment to the Constitution, which outlawed slavery. The 14th amendment gave blacks the rights of citizenship. The fight for lasting freedom to be truly equal members of this great democracy, however, continues today.

THE INTERNMENT OF JAPANESE AMERICANS DURING WORLD WAR II

America entered World War II on December 7, 1941, as a result of the attack on Pearl Harbor, Hawaii, by Japan. The attack killed several thousand Americans, crippled the Pacific Navy, and greatly wounded American pride. One result of the attack was deep mistrust of Americans of Japanese ancestry. This mistrust continued to build until it led to the *internment* (detention or confinement) of persons of Japanese ancestry, who

110,000 Japanese Americans were interned in secret camps on American soil during World War II.

Pictured here in 1943, the Manzanar Relocation Center in California and other internment camps for Japanese Americans were kept secret from the American public until after World War II ended in 1945.

were forced to move from their homes to camps until after the war had ended. Seventy-five percent of those interned were American citizens. Howard Zinn writes,

> After the Pearl Harbor attack, anti-Japanese hysteria spread in the government. One Congressman said: "I'm for catching every Japanese in America, Alaska and Hawaii now and putting them in concentration camps. . . . Damn them! Let's get rid of them!" Franklin D. Roosevelt did not share this frenzy, but he calmly signed Executive Order 9066 in February 1942, giving the army the power, without warrants or indictments or hearings, to arrest every Japanese-American on the West Coast—110,000 men, women, and children—to take them from their homes, transport them to camps far into the interior, and keep them there under prison conditions.[19]

It wasn't until the end of the war that the government let the American public know of the internment of Japanese Americans. Some Japanese Americans spent five years in these camps.

TO BE FREE

historical racism in Minnesota and Wisconsin

Insidious (sinister) racism isn't confined to the actions of national governments, or to events that happen in places far from where we live. Sometimes racial incidents happen right here in our state, in neighboring states, and in our local communities.

The Ojibwe homeland once extended over large portions of Michigan, Wisconsin, Minnesota, and parts of North Dakota. White settlers wanted the land opened to settlement so they could use it for agriculture. The soil was rich, and the settlers wanted to use it to plant and harvest crops. Eventually, through a series of treaties, the Ojibwe *ceded* (to surrender or give up) much of this land to the federal government. In exchange, they were to receive small payments, *annuities* (small yearly payments of cash, food, and goods), and supplies.

Still, there was pressure to open up even more land. To accomplish this, the government decided to move all Ojibwe people from Michigan, Wisconsin, and eastern Minnesota to land west of the Mississippi River. In 1850, Secretary of Interior Thomas Ewing and Commissioner of Indian Affairs Orlando Brown, along with Minnesota Territorial governor Alexander Ramsey and Sub-Agent John Watrous, plotted to lure the Ojibwe to Sandy Lake to issue payments and goods. (In previous years, distribution of annuities and goods had taken place at La Pointe, Wisconsin.) More than three thousand Ojibwe people gathered at Sandy Lake, in east central Minnesota, in October 1850. Hunger, disease, and exposure to the elements resulted in 170 deaths; another 270 died on their way home. In all, the plan that these politicians and federal agents designed led to the deaths of four hundred Ojibwe men, women, and children.

The memorial (mikwendaagoziwag) for the Ojibwe who died at Sandy Lake while awaiting for annuities.

The U.S.–Dakota War

For centuries the Dakota had flourished over much of Minnesota and Wisconsin. With the arrival of the Ojibwe in the seventeenth century, the Dakota were pushed out of Wisconsin and into the south and west of Minnesota. White settlers arrived soon thereafter. Eventually, the Dakota's homeland was confined by a series of treaties, beginning with the 1826 Treaty of Prairie du Chien, to land south of the Minnesota River, and continuing with the treaties of 1851 that ceded most of their remaining land in southern Minnesota. The Dakota were eventually confined to a small strip of land along the Minnesota River and plots of land south of the present-day Twin Cities. They also lost access to their sacred pipestone quarries at Pipestone, Minnesota. White settlers wanted what remained of the Dakota's prized potential farmland, and urged the U.S. government to get much of the remaining land ceded through treaties with the Dakota.

The Dakota ceded more than 24 million acres and were paid just over $3 million in cash and annuities. Much of the cash actually ended up in the hands of traders in the form of "trader's payments," and to *mixed-bloods* (people of Dakota and white ancestry), causing more mistrust among the Dakota. Other events heightened the tension between the Dakota and whites, including delays in the arrival of annuities and supplies promised by the government. Annuity payments and supplies were lost or never delivered due to corruption within the Bureau of Indian Affairs. This led to severe hunger and hardship for many Dakota, and they could see no immediate end to their suffering. For some, their only hope was to drive whites from the area that used to be their homeland.

The triggering event for the U.S.–Dakota War occurred when a group of Dakota killed five settlers near Grove City, in Meeker County. Under the leadership of Little Crow, the Dakota rose up against the settlers of the Minnesota River Valley in August 1862. By the end of the struggle, nearly five hundred white settlers and military personnel would be dead.[20] The number of Dakota eventually killed is unknown.

The Dakota were no match militarily against the guns and cannons of American military forces, and eventually surrendered near Montevideo, Minnesota. Hasty trials were held for those accused of partaking in the uprising, some trials lasting no more than five minutes. Three hundred and three Dakota were given death sentences; and while President Abraham Lincoln commuted the death sentences of 264 Dakota, thirty-eight were eventually hanged at Mankato in what remains the largest mass execution in U.S. history.

TO BE FREE

Indian jail holding Sioux uprising captives during the U.S.–Dakota War, 1862.

The other seventeen hundred Dakota women, children, and men who had surrendered were marched to Fort Snelling. Along the way white settlers attacked them with knives, guns, stones, and clubs. But the rage among Minnesotans about the killings was not over. They demanded the removal of all Dakota from Minnesota. Congress approved this removal in 1863, as well as the removal of the Winnebago people, some of whom had participated in the

uprising. Thirteen hundred Dakota and 1,950 Winnebago were forced from Minnesota to the Dakota and Nebraska territories. Eventually, however, some "friendly" Dakota were allowed to remain in Minnesota. Others returned in small bands.

The U.S.–Dakota War marked the beginning of years of armed conflict between the Dakota and Lakota people (those from Minnesota refer to themselves as Dakota and those from the Dakotas refer to themselves as Lakota) and American forces. Many American soldiers and Dakota and Lakota warriors died in the battles, as did innocent settlers and Dakota and Lakota people. Many thousands of Lakota people were displaced from their traditional homelands. The struggle would last for many years, ending with the massacre in 1890 of 190 Lakota, mostly women and children, at Wounded Knee, South Dakota. The great Oglala holy man, Black Elk, described the final scene at Wounded Knee:

It was a good winter day when all this happened. The sun was shining. But after the soldiers marched away from their dirty

One of the Indian victims of the massacre at Wounded Knee, 1890.

TO BE FREE

work, a heavy snow began to fall. The winds came up in the night. There was a big blizzard, and it grew very cold. The snow drifted deep in the crooked gulch, and it was one long grave of butchered women and children and babies, who had never done any harm and were only trying to run away.[21]

The lynchings in Duluth

Perhaps one of the ugliest racial incidents in Minnesota history was the 1920 lynching of three young black men in Duluth. The three were accused of raping a white girl—it was later found that the girl had lied. The young men were dragged from their jail cells by a mob of thousands of angry whites and hanged from city lampposts. In his book about the crime, *The Lynchings in Duluth*, author Michael Fedo describes the scene in chilling detail:

As the noose was adjusted around his neck, he shrieked, "God be with me. I'm not the right man." He was hoisted to his feet, and the rope was drawn up, but he fell when the rope loosened. A thin, short man near him tried choking McGhie [the victim], but was pulled back as the rope was refastened and McGhie was lifted up a few feet off the ground, just clear of the pavement. The crowd had pressed so close that as McGhie gasped in his death

The Clayton, Jackson, McGhie memorial in Duluth.

agony, blood blown from his parted lips spattered on the faces of those near him.[22]

News of the lynching was kept quiet for many years, while the three souls lay buried in unmarked graves in Duluth. Finally, in 2000, a group of people came together to build a lasting memorial for the three innocent, murdered young men.

From a speech given by Senator Barack Obama
at the Constitution Center
in Philadelphia, Pennsylvania, March 28, 2008

...I CHOSE TO RUN FOR THE PRESIDENCY at this moment in history because I believe deeply that we cannot solve the challenges of our time unless we solve them together—unless we perfect our union by understanding that we may have different stories, but we hold common hopes; that we may not look the same and we may not have come from the same place, but we all want to move in the same direction—towards a better future for our children and our grandchildren.

This belief comes from my unyielding faith in the decency and generosity of the American people. But it also comes from my own American story.

I am the son of a black man from Kenya and a white woman from Kansas. I was raised with the help of a white grandfather who survived a Depression to serve in Patton's Army during World War II and a white grandmother who worked on a bomber assembly line at Fort Leavenworth while he was overseas. I've gone to some of the best schools in America and lived in one of the world's poorest nations. I am married to a black American who carries within her the blood of slaves and slaveowners—an inheritance we pass on to our two precious daughters. I have brothers, sisters, nieces, nephews, uncles, and cousins of every race and every hue, scattered across three continents, and for as long as I live, I will never forget that in no other country on Earth is my story even possible....

The Clayton Jackson McGhie Memorial Committee (named in honor of the three young men) raised funds for a sculpture and small park near the site of the lynching. Today, students in Duluth's schools and other schools in Minnesota and Wisconsin learn about what happened not so many years ago, when racism took over the streets, and hearts, of one of our cities.

The Struggle

A lesson of history is that real change sometimes requires great patience. By knowing the history of racism in America, we also know that positive change has come about slowly. We are part of that change.

Still, change often seems so painfully slow. Langston Hughes' poem "A Dream Deferred" captures the frustration felt by so many who work their entire lives for racial justice, only to see it *elude* (to stay out of reach, escape) them:

WHAT HAPPENS TO A DREAM DEFERRED?
Does it dry up like a raisin in the sun?
Or fester like a sore—And then run?
Does it stink like rotten meat?
Or crust and sugar over—
like a syrupy sweet?
Maybe it just sags like a heavy load.
Or does it explode?

Some people who work to achieve racial equality call this work "The Struggle." To struggle means to continue to push, no matter how long or how difficult. To struggle means to acknowledge that the quest for equal rights is a difficult journey, with all kinds of roadblocks along the way. To struggle means to measure progress in small victories. To struggle assumes some of us will be overcome by self-doubt, setbacks, and sometimes by our own rage. To struggle means that we know injustices will continue to occur. We also know the struggle may take generations to establish true equality, requiring patience of such depth that one would think there was no more to give.

Why? The answer is simple.

TO BE FREE.

CHAPTER UNDERSTANDINGS

THEME

☞ **Racism** has had significant influence on the development of American society throughout history.

ACTIVITIES TO PROMOTE UNDERSTANDING

1. Do a library or Web search on a significant racial event in American or Minnesota history. Write or give an oral report to your peers on your findings. Make connections between the event and other events of the same historical period. For example, in what ways did many whites view people of color during the historical period you've chosen? What other racial events were occurring during that period? How were other communities of color (blacks, Native Americans, Asian Americans, Latinos) treated during the historical period you've chosen? Give examples or illustrations. How might history have been different if this event had not occurred?

2. Write a story or narrative from the perspective of an African slave aboard a slave ship to America, a young Japanese American internee during World War II, or a Native American being removed from his or her traditional homelands and forced onto a reservation by the government. Put yourself in their shoes. Include as much as you know from history in order to tell the story as accurately as possible. Finally, think of questions you still have about why the event occurred. What else do you need to know in order to accurately tell the story? Where might you look for additional information?

White privilege personified, 1935. How is white privilege still with us today?

unconscious, unintentional racism

THIS CHAPTER takes a look at something many adults (especially adults) have a difficult time understanding, much less accepting: white privilege and *unconscious* (not being aware), unintentional racism. What is "white privilege," a term that describes the advantages of being white in America? And what is unconscious, unintentional racism? Why do some white women clutch their purses when they come upon a group of black, Asian, Latino, or Native youth on the street? Why do some white men get nervous in a public restroom or an elevator full of black men? Why do so many whites have involuntary negative reactions when flashed *subliminal* (hidden) images of black faces in social experiments? And because people of color take notice when these things happen, in what ways might acts of unconscious, unintentional racism sometimes seem even more hurtful and degrading than in-your-face racism?

cowboys 24, indians 0

If we looked at life in America like it was a football game, the Cowboys (a silly metaphor for being white) would be spotted twenty-four points at the beginning of the game. No one said anything about that being fair. That's just the way it has been since America's beginning. And the weird thing is some Cowboys don't even recognize the advantages of being a Cowboy, thinking all along that life in America takes place on an even playing field, and that we begin the game of life zero to zero. The myth of an even playing field is like a fairy tale pounded in our heads, a fairy tale that tells us that everyone is equal and has equal opportunity.

Wrong.

So maybe we need to begin by giving white privilege a face, describing what it

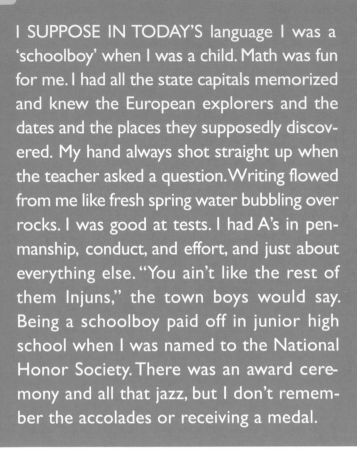

I SUPPOSE IN TODAY'S language I was a 'schoolboy' when I was a child. Math was fun for me. I had all the state capitals memorized and knew the European explorers and the dates and the places they supposedly discovered. My hand always shot straight up when the teacher asked a question. Writing flowed from me like fresh spring water bubbling over rocks. I was good at tests. I had A's in penmanship, conduct, and effort, and just about everything else. "You ain't like the rest of them Injuns," the town boys would say. Being a schoolboy paid off in junior high school when I was named to the National Honor Society. There was an award ceremony and all that jazz, but I don't remember the accolades or receiving a medal.

There was this teacher who considered himself a friend of the Indians. "Some of my best friends are Indians," he would say. He always reminded us that he was our defender at teacher meetings, against all the rednecks. We were like his pet Indians. If you are black, Native, Hmong, Latino, or whatever, maybe you know what I mean when I say that. Anyway, at the award ceremony he came up to me and told me something like this:

'I really had to fight to get you this award. See, we've never had an Indian on the National Honor Society before.'

That's what I remember.

looks and feels like. First, in order to begin understanding what white privilege is, it's important to tuck away any white guilt anyone may be feeling. Put it away. Pass it on. White guilt is a privilege. Think about it: Do black, Native, Latinos, or Asian Americans feel guilty for being who they are? No.

Next, it might help to approach this difficult topic with a sense of humor, even though it is very serious. Sometimes a sense of humor helps. This topic is like a tough hill to climb. Like a raging river to ford.

Like something we need to get through in order to get over. So let's begin.

Let's say you are sitting in seventh period history, Friday afternoon before Christmas break, studying the framers of the Constitution, the founding fathers. See any black founding fathers there? Crazy Horse? Sitting Bull? Anyone Chinese? Anyone from Latin America? You can be sure all the founding fathers were white, and males in this case as well, because only white male landowners had the right to

TO BE FREE

All of the founding fathers were white males.
Only white male landowners could participate in government.

vote when our American democracy was established. When "We the People" was written, it didn't include many of us; women, men who weren't property owners, and people of color were purposefully excluded. Whole populations of people had to wait a while, some a long, long while, before they were included as "We."

Cowboys up by seven.

"We're an English-speaking country," we've been hearing on the news. Local and state governments are proposing English-only laws. Nothing wrong with that, I suppose, most of us are probably thinking. A common language makes it easier for all of us to communicate, and good communication is at the heart of everything we do—work, school, life.

But what message does "English-only" send to those whose first language is Spanish, Thai, Arabic, or Mandarin? What about all the Native languages like Dakota, Ho-Chunk, or Ojibwe that are in danger of extinction? Aren't they the original American languages?

The message sent in the English-only proposals isn't even subtle: other languages aren't as valued. We will all speak and write English because that is *the way*, the right way. And while we're at it, some are saying, let's put the National Guard at

our southern border to keep *them* out.

Cowboys up by fourteen.

White people can offer their opinions on something and not have their opinions interpreted as representing all white people. No one will ever ask, "So what do you (white) people think?" White people

Poster in a store window.

TO BE FREE

The border wall separating the U.S. from Mexico in Nogales, Arizona in 2006.

will never hear anyone ask them questions like: How much is that (white) casino making, anyway? Do you (white) people pay taxes? How come you (white) people are always together?

In most places—stores, schools, on the street, at a Packers or Brewers or Twins or Vikings game—the majority of the crowd will be those with their same ethnic background. Most of the television programs will be about people whose ethnic background matches theirs. Most of the elected members of city councils, school boards, county boards, state legisla-

tures, and the federal government are white. If there are black or Asian or Latino or Native elected members, they will often be called upon to speak for "their people." "What do your people think?" they will hear time and time again. They will be put on all the diversity and Equal Opportunity committees. They will be asked to come along when the mayor or governor or senator visits black or Native or Somali or Hmong communities.

In predominately white neighborhoods, white people aren't thought of as the "white neighbors."

No one will say the smell of their cooking is all over the neighborhood. No one will say they drive a "white" car. No one will stare at their reservation's license plates. Most will be able to go into a store and not feel they are being followed around or harassed because they are white. If they go into a convenience store to buy a candy bar and find they don't have enough money, they won't think the clerk is thinking, "Those white people can't even come up with the money to buy a candy bar."

Their parents didn't have to teach them to be wary of societal racism against whites, of store clerks or police or teachers who may judge them based solely on the color of their skin. Their mothers will never warn them to be careful when speaking up against an alleged injustice by authority figures, especially the police. They don't have to worry about finding Band-Aids that match their skin or makeup, or hairdressers who know how to do their hair. They won't have to search high and low in grocery stores for food that fits their ethnic heritage. If they do well, they won't be told they are "a credit to the white race." Most won't have to worry about being called schoolboys or schoolgirls by their white peers. They will never have to worry about learning to speak proper Ojibwe or Dakota or Mandarin in order to buy a burger

and fries or to ask for directions.

They will never be tested about their knowledge of Hmong or Somali or Native history to earn their high school diploma. Their ethnic background will never show as a spelling error when using a spellchecker on the computer. They will never have to defend themselves in court against challenges from the very states in which they are citizens to retain their treaty rights, or to hunt and fish in the land of their ancestors. They will never be called "wagon burners." They will never have to fight to change the names of sports teams called the Whitemen or the Whiteys, and thus will never have to listen to arguments that such names are really respectful of whites and that those who want the names changed are being too "politically correct."

Most whites are able to criticize the government without being called a "militant" or "dissident" or a "minority activist." They will not have to worry about the fire department or an ambulance hesitating to respond to a call in their neighborhood. They can go to the golf course, Kiwanis meetings, Boy and Girl Scouts, Daughters of the American Revolution gatherings, or just about anywhere without feeling out of place or like they are the only one, or the few. In golf tournaments, they will never be called a "white golfer."

TO BE FREE

They won't have an asterisk after their name in the record books if they break home run records. If they get a good job or promotion, no one will say they got it just because of Affirmative Action. If they are a bad leader, no one will say it's because they're white. If they think about running for president, their husbands or wives won't plead with them not to run because they are terrified someone will assassinate them because they are white.

If they are late for school, or for any meeting for that matter, the people waiting for them will not think all whites are habitually late. If they are writers, they won't be labeled as a "minority" voice. Their works won't be put in the "ethnic" shelves of bookstores. Their poetry and stories won't be published in "white" anthologies. They won't have a television program that only airs at six in the morning, on public television, when most people are asleep, called "White People Today."

As whites, they will even be afforded privilege among groups of color. They can go to pow-wows with a Native friend, who will teach them all about Native tradition, and come away having learned as much or more about Native tradition than most Native kids learn in schools. Their opinions will be given more *credence* (authority) in an audience of people of color, even more so than blacks or Asians or Latinos or Natives who have more expertise than they do. They will never feel they aren't normal.

Cowboys up by twenty-one.

And finally, if white people don't think white privilege exists, they won't be discredited for it. For that, we can tag on a field goal. Cowboys ahead, 24-0.

The game is about to begin.

NERVOUS AS A PUPPY

Well, maybe not that nervous. Some adults, however, get plenty nervous when they come upon a group of young black or Latino or Asian or Native kids on the street. Some do the clutch-and-grab (their kids, if they are tagging along, or their purses or handbags). Others do the avoid-eye-contact-at-all-costs thing, or the cross-the-street thing, or the pick-up-the-pace thing.

The young people, about whom the adults are so nervous, notice what's going on. To them, these reactions are degrading. It happens all the time. It is painful to think that others view them as a bunch of criminals. And the thing is, people who get all nervous like that, most all of them don't have an in-your-face racist bone in their bodies. So what's to get all uptight about then?

The nervous response I am referring to is unconscious or unintentional racism.

Getting nervous like that isn't just something white adults do. Many of us have been *conditioned* (trained, miseducated) to get nervous around people from other ethnic groups, especially young males. We've heard stories about tough "Asian gangs" or black kids, and so on, all of our lives. These stereotypes have been pounded in our heads by television and movies. As a young Native, I was told to be wary around authority figures, especially the police.

"Don't you ever talk back to them," we were warned. "They'll beat you." And so I grew up being afraid of the police. As far as I was concerned, the police were there to beat on Indians.

The same thing goes with store clerks. "You watch them 'cause they're watching you. Don't even *think* about stealin'." So I grew up thinking that store clerks weren't there to help customers; they were there to watch Indians so we wouldn't steal anything.

How is the misinformation and stereotyping that leads to unconscious, unintentional racism spread? Dr. Beverly Daniel Tatum explains:

The impact of racism begins early. Even in our preschool years, we are exposed to misinformation about people different

> IF YOU AS PARENTS CUT CORNERS, YOUR CHILDREN WILL TOO. IF YOU LIE, THEY WILL TOO.... AND IF PARENTS SNICKER AT RACIAL AND GENDER JOKES, ANOTHER GENERATION WILL PASS ON THE POISON ADULTS STILL HAVE NOT HAD THE COURAGE TO SNUFF OUT.
>
> MARIAN WRIGHT EDELMAN

TO BE FREE

from ourselves. Many of us grew up in neighborhoods where we had limited opportunities to interact with people different from our own families. When I ask my college students, "How many of you grew up in neighborhoods where most of the people were from the same racial group as your own?" almost every hand goes up. There is still a great deal of social segregation in our communities. Consequently, most of the early information we receive about "others"—people racially, religiously, or socioeconomically different from ourselves—does not come as the result of first hand experience. The second hand information we do receive has often been distorted, shaped by cultural stereotypes, and left incomplete.[23]

bull circle

Getting nervous in an elevator full of black men is a result of misinformation, stereotypes that have been ingrained in the thinking of many non-black people for generations. Becoming nervous when seeing a group of black or Asian or Native or Latino youths approaching is the result of misinformation, of images force-fed to us by the media (television, movies and videos, newspapers and magazines). These stereotypes are also the result of exaggerations and biased reports

passed down from person to person, like gossip, until the exaggerations become truth, until myth becomes law.

Sometimes unconscious, unintentional racism exposes itself in subtle, hurtful ways. It rears its

Interpreters for recent immigrants help to bridge language, cultural, and religious gaps between people.

ugly head when we find ourselves laughing at ethnic jokes, even though we know it is wrong to do so. Even more telling, it is present when we hear others tell ethnic jokes and don't laugh, yet say nothing. It is present when we witness injustices—when we know full well that people of color are ignored in a school's curriculum and do nothing about it, or when we say nothing to the blatant, in-your-face racists we hear spreading lies about people of color.

Unconscious, unintentional racism occurs when we believe we live in a "color-blind" society, where everybody is treated alike, no matter their color, all the while ignoring the evidence that says otherwise. Unconscious, unintentional racism is ingrained in our language: "At the bottom of the totem pole"; "Sitting like an Indian"; "What a Jew." Can you think of more?

None of this means we are bad people. Whites are not bad. Asians are not bad. Blacks are not bad. Latinos are not bad. Natives are not bad. But we need to change.

How do we begin to change all of this? We begin by *acknowledging* (admitting, accepting) that racism exists, and that it is deeply woven into our culture in all its forms. We begin by acknowledging that white privilege exists, and that change will happen only when we actively work to change things for the better. It is our decision to make. And although it is a simple, just, difficult, painful, necessary decision to make,

WE WILL BE A BETTER PEOPLE AS A RESULT.

WE WILL BE FREE.

The Nazis forced Jewish people to wear the Star of David, which publicly identified them as Jews.

CHAPTER UNDERSTANDINGS

THEMES

☞ **There are inherent** (built-in) privileges of being white (white privilege) in America.

☞ **Unconscious, unintentional racism** results from misinformation and stereotypes about people of color.

ACTIVITIES TO PROMOTE UNDERSTANDING

1. There are other privileges besides white privilege—being slender, smart, athletic, *articulate* (a good speaker), more social (maybe you make friends easily) than most, to name but a few. Think of all the privileges you can and list them. Now, think of areas where *you* might have privilege where others do not. What are they? Share them with your peers.

2. Create a dialogue between two people about an incident regarding white privilege. Use one of the examples given in the chapter or come up with one on your own.

3. Do research about the English-only debate going on in our country. In what ways is the debate related to the issue of illegal immigration? Are certain groups being targeted in our efforts to stem the tide of illegal immigration?

4. Ethnic jokes were discussed as an example of unconscious, unintentional racism because they can seem such an *imbedded* (common) part of American culture. What are your views about telling ethnic jokes? When, if ever, is it appropriate to tell ethnic jokes? How do you react to ethnic jokes? Is there any difference between ethnic jokes and jokes about the blind, mentally handicapped, overweight, blond, or others? Why is it that people of color sometimes tell (and some professional comedians in fact make their living) telling ethnic jokes about people of their own ethnic group?

Native children were sent to boarding schools where they were forbidden to speak their language.

chapter five

THE MISSING STORIES

THERE WAS A TIME in America when most people believed that new immigrants should totally transform into Americans, that they should adopt American culture—language, clothing, music, art, beliefs—and become *assimilated* (to learn, absorb, become a part of). Immigrants would no longer use their languages, but learn to speak and write in English. Their old ways would be discarded.

At the same time, Native children were being sent to boarding and mission schools, where they were forbidden to speak their languages and were removed from their cultures. The belief that everyone should become alike was known as the "melting pot myth." According to the melting pot myth, if everyone was alike, then everyone would be equal. America would be not be divided by differences.

Yet many immigrants settled in places where other people like them lived, others who shared their language and culture. Ethnic restaurants, stores, churches, synagogues, and mosques sprang up in these neighborhoods and communities. Some communities published their own newspapers and

Temple Israel in Minneapolis, c. 1890.

67

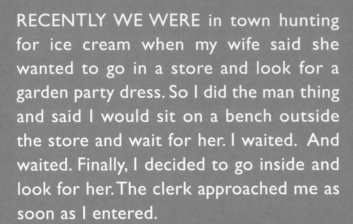

RECENTLY WE WERE in town hunting for ice cream when my wife said she wanted to go in a store and look for a garden party dress. So I did the man thing and said I would sit on a bench outside the store and wait for her. I waited. And waited. Finally, I decided to go inside and look for her. The clerk approached me as soon as I entered.

'May I help you?'

'My wife is here, somewhere,' I said.

'No, I don't think so,' she said. I could tell by her voice that I was unwelcome.

'Well, maybe she is upstairs or in the changing room,' I said.

'No,' she said, 'she isn't here. There is no one upstairs.' And she walked me to the door.

I'm sure many of you think what happened was nothing. But I know the look and feel and voice of prejudice. I have seen and felt and known it nearly sixty years. Now, approaching being an elder, overeducated in mainstream schools, I will always have these little incidences to serve as reminders that no matter my official role in society, I am still a dirty, sneaky Injun to some.

magazines in their own languages, and broadcast programs over the radio and television in their own languages. At the same time, the government separated Native people and forced them onto reservations. So even though many believed the melting pot effect would smooth out differences, or eliminate them, people actually kept many of their old ways. In addition, some immigrants realized that no matter how hard they tried to assimilate into American culture, they were never fully accepted. Latinos, Natives, Asian Americans, and blacks continued to be treated poorly.

Because some ethnic groups wanted to retain their cultures and ways, and because many were never fully accepted into the American mainstream despite their efforts, the melting pot myth became just that—a myth. Nowadays, some think of the great diversity in our country more as a mosaic. A mosaic is a wonderful blend of different colors and textures, each adding to the beauty of the whole. A diversity of cultures is like a mosaic: people keep parts of their cultures—their languages, food, music, and religions—while, at the same time, being Americans they try to be part of the great American story.

Institutional Racism

This way of looking at America's great diversity as a mosaic, however, is sometimes slow to catch on in institutions. Racism may exist in the ways institutions, such as schools, governments, hospitals, and museums operate. These ways include: rules, policies, staffing, laws, values, and accepted ways of doing things. This racism may take many forms, including: intentional, unconscious, and unintentional racism.

As institutions, schools are given the responsibility of educating. Sometimes in schools, however, there are inequalities when it comes to what is or isn't taught. The story of people of color may be missing. Or the story may be only partially told, or what is told may be incorrect. The story includes the histories, cultures, languages, art, philosophies (ways of thinking), and literature of a people.

Something else may also be missing from schools: people. There may be few teachers, administrators, or school board members who are people of color. People of color may work primarily in jobs like custodians, secretaries, and aides. The school rules and policies may clash with the culture of diverse ethnic groups. The pictures, displays, hallways, and bulletin boards may lack representation of people from diverse ethnic groups. Teachers may have little or no background or training about the cultures of the different ethnic groups to which their students belong, so they may lack the knowledge or understanding to include information about the different cultures in their teaching or in the ways they teach. All of these things are examples of institutional racism.

Missing Stories

Sometimes the stories we are taught excludes a group. Jaime, a Seneca from New York, had something to say about what was *not* included in his classes:

> It's all about Americans, not Native Americans, just plain Americans. That's all. That's all they teach us, nothing about Native Americans. It's like they always talk about the wars and stuff, how the Indians did all this stuff. I'd like to teach American history. I'd like to teach it myself so that I could get up in front of the class and tell a lot of students what really happened.[24]

Some schools and many teachers do include the perspectives of people of color in their teaching. Many, however, do not. Part of the reason for this is because diversity and acknowledging different points of view, knowledge, skills, and understandings was not a part of their teacher training. In addition, many texts used in our schools do not include much content from a diverse perspective.

Schools generally do not teach students about art from the great Eastern civilizations of China, India, and Japan.

The result is that some classrooms lack a diverse perspective. Oftentimes in social studies classes, much of the time devoted to studying early American history is spent on the colonizing of the country by Europeans, with small units on Native, black, Asian, or Latino history, if they are included at all. The history of Western civilization (Europe and the ancient Greeks and Romans) may be favored over any study of the great Eastern civilizations in China, India, or Japan, or the great civilizations in the Americas, such as the Incan or Mayan kingdoms.

In other subject areas, the same narrow perspective may persist. Art studies may include only Western (mainstream American and European, Greek, and Roman) art. The great European artists and their works are studied, but the art of China, Japan, Africa, and of Native people may be ignored. In music classes, mainstream music and musical instruments may be favored over the music and instruments of other cultures. If they are included at all, the music will often be labeled "ethnic" music. In literature classes, the writings of great authors from China, Japan, the Middle East, and Africa are not generally included in the curriculum. The same is true in the study of philosophy, in which teachers may devote most classroom time to the works of Greek philosophers like Socrates, Aristotle, and Plato, and barely touch

TO BE FREE

on the ideas of great Eastern philosophers like Chuang-Tzu, a great Chinese philosopher. The teaching of other subjects, such as science, mathematics, and the performing arts may also suffer from a lack of diverse perspective.

At other times, misconceptions about people of color persist because of a lack of knowledge. Dr. Beverly Daniel Tatum explains:

> Sometimes the *assumptions* [something believed without proof] we make about others come not from what we have been told or what we have seen on television or in books, but rather from what we have *not* been told. The distortion of historical information about people of color leads young people (and older people, too) to make assumptions that go unchallenged for a long time. Consider this conversation between two white students following a discussion about the cultural *transmission* [the spread] of racism:
>
> "Yeah, I just found out that Cleopatra was actually a Black woman."
>
> "What?"
>
> The first student went on to explain her newly learned information. The second student explained in disbelief, "That can't be true. Cleopatra is beautiful!"[25]

Cleopatra (69 B.C. – 30 B.C.) was an African woman.

half-done stories

This issue is more difficult to understand because teachers are actually trying to teach their students about people of color. They are well meaning. However, too little is being done to educate young people about the history of people of color, so when teachers do touch upon this history, their efforts are seen as *tokenism* (a small gesture, regarded as minimal).

Authors Pamela L. Tiedt and Iris M. Tiedt have described some examples of tokenism in their writings. These examples, which I've paraphrased below, include:

When stories and histories about people of color are only taught during special holidays (such as the study of Native Americans only during Thanksgiving, the study of black authors only during Black History Month, reading about Dr. Martin Luther King, Jr. only near his birthday, or serving egg rolls in the school cafeteria only during the Chinese New Year). How do we know when schools are doing enough?

When a classroom has one or only a few books that are about blacks, Asians, Native Americans, or Latinos, among many other books, or only one or a few pictures of people of color on the walls. How many books or pictures are enough? The answer to that question may be when no one notices how few books in the bookshelves are by people of color, or how few pictures on the walls are of people of different ethnicities.

When what is taught about people of color focuses mainly on the past or presents them mainly as victims. Examples include when the study of black history only includes slavery, or when Native history includes only the period when Native people lost their homelands to white settlers. What else should students learn about from their teachers? We should learn not just about the past, but also about people as they are now, today, and tomorrow.

When materials about specific countries (Mexico, Liberia, Cambodia, and China, for example) are used to teach students about people of color in the United States. Americans of all ethnic groups are often very different from the people from the countries of their ancestors—the countries of their parents, grandparents, and great-grandparents.

Culture Conflicts

Sometimes classroom rules don't fit all cultures. A teacher may have a rule, for example, that says, "Look at me when I'm talking to you." In some cultures, however, looking at another person directly may not be appropriate. Or a teacher may give points to students for volunteering answers in class; but some cultures value more *reserved* (quiet, not volunteering) behavior. So a student from that culture has to decide which rules—the culture's or the school's—to observe.

At other times school holidays follow mainstream

Dr. Martin Luther King, Jr. speaking in St. Paul in 1967.

religious traditions. The traditional holiday break coincides with Christmas. Other cultures celebrate their religious holidays at different times of the year. Schools sometimes celebrate Columbus Day, a day that celebrates the European explorer who is not recognized as a hero in many Native communities. Sometimes, the content of classes might cause a culture clash when a cultural value conflicts with mainstream values. For example, in biology class, a student may be required to dissect a frog. However, in some Native cultures, frogs are believed to have a soul spirit, and are an equal or superior being to humankind. In Ojibwe culture, animals are considered elder brothers.

full circle

Schools don't disregard diverse cultures and those cultures' values on purpose. Sometimes schools have a difficult time finding and hiring teachers and administrators of color. Many teachers have had little training about teaching from a diverse perspective. And so culture clashes are often the result of simply not knowing.

But sometimes just talking about racial issues can be uncomfortable for both students and teachers. Dr. Beverly Daniel Tatum writes,

> As one elementary teacher said: "It is hard to tell small children about slavery, hard to explain that young black men were lynched and that police turned hoses on children while others bombed churches, killing black children at their prayers. This history is a terrible legacy for all

Accepting one another with our differences makes for a peaceful and happy society.

of us. The other day [another] teacher told me that she could not look into the faces of her students when she taught about these things. It was too painful and too embarrassing."[26]

Schools should observe and respect the culture, values, and heritage of the diverse people in our nation. Even if it is uncomfortable, teachers need to talk about the painful history of race relations in our country and remind students of how much we have overcome since the times of slavery, or internment, or being forced onto reservations. And students need to also know, through specific examples, that throughout history all whites weren't bad. Many helped people of color overcome the prejudice of the past.

We have come such a long way. We have a way to go. Many schools *reflect* (mirror, imitate) mainstream (white) culture. If we believe that America is truly a mosaic, our schools should reflect that belief. Parents and the community share equally in this responsibility.

TO BE FREE

CHAPTER UNDERSTANDINGS

THEMES

☞ **Racism** sometimes exists in the ways that institutions like schools, governments, hospitals, and museums function.

☞ **The stories** of people of color are sometimes missing, only partially told, or told inaccurately in many schools.

☞ **Cultural conflict** can occur when there is *incongruence* (disagreements, differences) between institutional culture and an individual's culture.

ACTIVITIES TO PROMOTE UNDERSTANDING

1. Select an ethnic group for study—black, Latino, Native, Asian American, or any other ethnic group. In small groups, do research (library and/or Web searches) on one thing that could be taught in schools to acknowledge the group's history, culture, language, art, philosophy, or literature. Prepare a short presentation to teach your peers about it.

2. Here are some ideas. Select one and focus on it: Imagine if young people ruled in schools and adults were the students. What subjects would young people teach? How would they teach these subjects? What would the school culture—its values, beliefs, and ways of being—look like? Or imagine if young people and adults shared power in how schools were run, what was taught, and how it was taught. What might schools look like? Or, imagine even further if schools were designed around Ojibwe, Hmong, Dakota, or Somali cultures.

3. Imagine you just moved from Earth to a different planet. It is your first day of school on this new planet and you notice differences from your culture and the school's culture. What kinds of culture conflict might you experience? Will you change to better fit in, or will the school change so you feel more at home?

4. From your own perspective, why is race and racism sometimes so hard to talk about? Are there ways of making it an easier topic for discussion? What might be the consequences of talking openly about it? Or not talking about it? What topic in racism makes you most uncomfortable?

Demonstrators protesting the use of Indian mascots in sports team names.

in-your-face racism

SOMETIMES RACISM is *overt* (obvious, out in the open, clear), right in your face, raw, angry, teasing, and uncompromising. And when you can see, hear, feel, and almost taste and smell it, you are often surprised, no matter how many times you've seen it or experienced it yourself. In-your-face racism comes from all directions: through the media, in sports, in schools, as jokes told between friends. And it doesn't just come from the mouths of strangers. Sometimes it comes from people you know, trust, and even love.

STEREOTYPES

Stereotypes are labels that are applied to a whole group of people. When stereotypes are directed against a particular racial group, it is racism. Fill in the blank of these examples:

"_____ are lazy."

"_____ are drunks."

"_____ are all criminals."

"_____ don't pay taxes."

"_____ are simple-minded."

Now try to write down all the stereotypes you can think of that are used to describe certain groups of people. How many did you think of? How do you think these stereotypes originated?

Stereotypes are based on ignorance, misinformation, and lies. Even "good" stereotypes (thinking that all Asians are good at math, for example, or that blacks are better athletes) are wrong because no single label can be used to describe a whole group of people.

SPORTS MASCOTS

Some years ago, before Minnesota banned the use of American Indian mascots in sports team names, I was at a hockey game between my hometown "Lumberjacks" and the visiting "Indians."

FOR A WHILE we were living in St. Petersburg, Florida. St. Petersburg is a beautiful city on Florida's Gulf Coast. Right in downtown St. Petersburg, next to a marina, is a statue of Christopher Columbus, who is credited for "discovering" America. Columbus Day is a federal holiday in this country to honor him. The plaque under the statue has all kinds of wonderful things to say about the man.

We now know full well, of course, that Columbus didn't discover anything. When he first stepped ashore, the American continents were already populated by millions of Native people, people he erroneously called "Indians." And many of us Native people know the real story about Columbus, taken word for word from his own journal and the journals kept by the Jesuit missionaries who traveled with him. The journals tell how the Native people he "discovered" were wantonly slaughtered and enslaved by Columbus and his followers. Not by the hundreds, or thousands, but by the millions.

So anyway, back to St. Petersburg, Florida. Some time ago when my wife and I were walking past the statue of Columbus, she (normally mild-mannered and law-abiding) said something to the effect of, "We should push that thing over."

We will probably never do that, but in our hearts I suppose it would feel good, for just that moment, to see the statue toppled—as if doing it would bring to an end all the lies taught as truths about Columbus. As if wishing what happened five hundred years ago would have never occurred in the first place.

I imagine the news of our misdeed in the *St. Petersburg Times,* the local newspaper. The headline would read, "Indians Push Over Columbus."

That should have happened five hundred years ago.

(As a Native person, I've come to accept the term "Indian," even though the term is inaccurate.) The "Indians" cheerleaders were wearing cute pink headdresses. Some of the "Lumberjacks" fans were yelling racial *slurs* (insulting comments).

"SCALP THEM INJUNS!"
"KILL THEM WAGON BURNERS!"

Slurs, like those I overheard at the hockey game, are why Minnesota eventually banned the use of Indian mascots in school sports teams. While Minnesota and other states have led the nation in banning the use of Indian nicknames and mascots in sports, not all states or professional sports team owners have caught on.

Professor Denise Sweet, an Anishinaabe (Ojibwe) from White Earth, Minnesota, and Wisconsin's Poet Laureate, wrote about the anger and pain of watching Indian mascots on sports television programs in her poem "Indian War":

> It's hard enough to make simple talk of this
> Watching turkey feathers and greasepaint grins
> Dance akimbo upon the TV screen, The painted quarter horses carrying costumed braves, the rider screaming as though aflame.
> I'm disgusted about what I would like to say—

> The hurtful words I learned from punks—
> None will fit neatly into the fatness of gratitude
> You're expecting to hear from your Indians
> The ones you honor at half-time.[27]

There are some who would argue that we shouldn't change team names that feature Indian mascots; these people would say we are being "too politically correct." (Politically correct is a term sometimes used to challenge the ideas of those who fight for civil rights, religious tolerance, and gender equality.) After all, some Native people aren't offended by the use of Indian mascots in sports. Many others, however, are offended. The people who are offended by the use of Indian names and mascots feel strongly that we do not honor Native people by naming a team the Washington Redskins or by doing the "tomahawk chop" of the Atlanta Braves. Maybe we should stop using phrases like "politically correct," which distract us from things that are really hurting people, and start making decisions simply based on whether something is right or wrong.

Racial Profiling

After the events of September 11, 2001, our country increased airport security in hopes of preventing future terrorists from hijacking planes and using them as weapons against us. Since then, some people of Middle Eastern descent have accused airport security of singling them out for greater scrutiny, such as inspections and searches, because the 9/11 terrorists were of Middle Eastern descent.

In other situations, black, Native, and Latino communities have accused some police officers of harassing them or singling them out. Blacks driving in "white" neighborhoods talk of being pulled over and asked where they are going. Natives complain of being pulled over by police, who run "routine" checks for violations. Others claim that store security monitors people of color more closely. Singling out a group based on race is called racial profiling.

Why is racial profiling so offensive? Most people of all ethnicities are law-abiding. When the police, airport security, or store security single out people of color, they are making wrong assumptions that people of color are more likely to be committing criminal acts. Have you ever been wrongfully accused or suspected of doing something wrong when you were innocent? If you have, then you can imagine how it feels to be a target of racial profiling. The Fourth Amendment to the U.S. Constitution prohibits unreasonable searches. The Fourteenth Amendment to the Constitution also guarantees that all citizens are to be treated equally under the law.

OVERT RACISM IN SCHOOLS

Let's face it: kids can sometimes be pretty mean to one another. Author Nancy Butcher, a woman of Japanese and white background, told how one day on the playground another little girl she often played with came up to her and said, "You caused Pearl Harbor."

Nancy didn't even know what Pearl Harbor was, and didn't realize, until a few years later in a history class, that her friend was referring to the Japanese attack on American forces at Pearl Harbor, Hawaii, in December 1941.

But one of Nancy's most painful memories is of what happened when her other classmates discovered her ethnicity:

> Once the word was officially out that I was half Japanese, I never heard the end of it from my classmates. They began calling me "Chink," squinting their eyes and bowing whenever they saw me, and yelling "Ah-So!" I was devastated and humiliated by this, but determined not to show it, and so I simply smiled every time I got teased.[28]

Nancy Butcher's experience in school is not uncommon among people of color or from mixed ethnic backgrounds. Sometimes, the racism even

TO BE FREE

comes from authority figures. Celeste, a Seneca Indian from New York, encountered racism from one of her teachers:

It was American History in the 11th grade, and the teacher wrote, "All Native Americans turned to alcoholism to ease their pain," and she put it all in like big letters and underlined it twice, and I said that was @!%&*. And I walked out, and then I got suspended for three days, and she didn't even have to apologize to me or nothing. Then when I played softball, well, I don't play anymore because I missed one practice, and they called me an alcoholic.[29]

Joyce Yuki Nakamura, a Japanese American girl, at Manzanar Relocation Center in 1943.

ETHNIC JOKES

There must be thousands of ethnic jokes—about the Irish, Finns, Poles, Italians, blacks, Natives, Asians, Latinos, Jews, and others. Finns, Poles, and Italians are often portrayed as simple-minded. Natives are sometimes portrayed as lazy or drunks, or "on the warpath." Jews might be portrayed as tight with their money. Jokes about blacks often focus on physical characteristics. Often, ethnic jokes are built on stereotypes and use humor at the expense of a whole class of people. And on the rare occasions the joke-teller is confronted about his or her poor taste in humor, most often the reply will attempt to turn the blame back on the person who confronted him or her: "Hey, I didn't mean any harm. It's just a joke. Gee, where's your sense of humor?"

Ethnic jokes are a form of in-your-face racism, particularly when they are told by someone from another ethnic group. Why is that? Here is an example: When Native people tell jokes about Natives, part of the joking may be a form of teasing. Teasing is a big thing in many Native communities. Humor and teasing are used as ways of giving advice or *admonishing* (telling off, reprimanding) someone. Joking also may be a form of "survival humor." Sometimes Native people use humor to mask or cope with life's difficulties.

However, when a white person tells a joke that pokes fun at Natives, the joke takes on a different tone. It is generally *not* funny because it may be perceived as a put-down. Many Native people have suffered from racism and are very sensitive when the joke is told by someone in mainstream culture. The feeling is similar to when a non-relative is making fun of your brother or sister—it's okay when you do it, but not okay when an outsider does it.

Ethnic jokes are sometimes told by people we trust and sometimes by those we love. Maybe Grandpa tells ethnic jokes. Maybe Uncle and Dad trade ethnic jokes. Your best friend may tell them. However, like all prejudice, jokes that are based on race are based on ignorance. And sometimes it's hard when we hear these jokes coming from people we really care about. We don't want to hurt their feelings by telling them the joke is inappropriate. We don't want to laugh because that wouldn't be appropriate either. And if we do laugh at the jokes, we might feel a bit guilty because in our hearts we know it isn't right.

What should you do when someone you love tells an ethnic joke? The right thing to do, and the most uncomfortable, is to tell the person the joke is inappropriate. This should be done privately, between you and the person who told the joke. If the teller is an elder (grandpa, dad, mother, uncle), you should speak to them in a way that is appropriate in your culture.

White Supremacists

White supremacist groups like the Ku Klux Klan, The Order, Posse Comitatus, and Aryan Nations all believe that white people are superior to people of different ethnic backgrounds. They believe people of color and Jews are inferior. While small in number, these groups have a history of violence directed against people different from themselves. Unfortunately, like the terrorists involved in 9/11, these groups have used their religious beliefs to justify their intolerance. Many of these groups believe God wants the people from different ethnic backgrounds to live separate from one another, that

A Ku Klux Klan meeting in St. Paul in 1922.

A NATIVE AMERICAN ELDER ONCE DESCRIBED HIS OWN INNER STRUGGLES IN THIS MANNER:

"INSIDE OF ME THERE ARE TWO DOGS. ONE OF THE DOGS IS MEAN AND EVIL, THE OTHER DOG IS GOOD. THE MEAN DOG FIGHTS THE GOOD DOG ALL THE TIME."

WHEN ASKED WHICH DOG WINS, HE REFLECTED FOR A MOMENT AND REPLIED,

"THE ONE I FEED THE MOST."

GEORGE BERNARD SHAW

apart is God's divine purpose. For example, the Aryan Nations would separate the North American continent into segregated regions. The states of Washington, Oregon, Montana, Wyoming, and Idaho would be for whites. The Hawaiian Islands would be reserved for Asians. California, Arizona, New Mexico, and most of Texas would be set aside for Mexican Americans. Long Island and Manhattan in New York would become the homeland of the Jews.

White supremacist organizations like the Klan play on ignorance and fear to try to convince others to believe in their racist beliefs. They try to get others to believe in negative stereotypes, especially those directed against blacks and Jews. They use their religious beliefs to promote the lie of racial superiority.

ḟull circle

On one hand it is easy to discredit the racist beliefs of supremacists as coming from a small group of "crazies." We would like to think the days of racial segregation have passed, that interracial dating and mixed marriages are acceptable with everyone, and that we live in a land that embraces diversity and equality for all. Somewhere along the road to equality, however, we have managed to divide racism into degrees, with the "crazies" on one extreme end and ethnic

white people are favored and people of color are "mud peoples."

To these hate groups, white supremacy is God's will, and keeping people from different groups

TO BE FREE

jokes on the other, with stereotyping and racial profiling somewhere in the middle.

The truth is that all forms of racism are equally harmful. All racism is based on ignorance, misinformation, and lies. All racism hurts to the bone.

RECOGNIZING THIS TRUTH WILL SET US FREE!

CHAPTER UNDERSTANDINGS

THEMES

☞ **Racism** is sometimes overt, in your face.

☞ **Overt racism** is present in stereotyping, team mascots, racial profiling, sometimes in schools, ethnic jokes, and in the beliefs of white supremacists.

ACTIVITIES TO PROMOTE UNDERSTANDING

1. On your own, write down as many stereotypes as you can think of about other people. Then go to the board and write them down. You might be surprised how many stereotypes your class comes up with. Listing them is a good jumping-off point for a discussion on stereotypes.

2. Do a Web search of "Indian mascots" for information on the opposing views regarding the use of Indian mascots in sports teams. Divide the class into small groups, each taking a position of either opposing or favoring the use of Indian mascots. Have each group present its findings to the class.

3. Imagine you work at a local airport for the TSA (Transportation Security Administration), the governmental organization in charge of our country's airport security. What kinds of people do you think might be targeted for closer security scrutiny? Why? Who do you think decides what kinds of people will be subject to closer scrutiny?

4. If you could change one thing about schools to make them less prone to overt, in-your-face acts of racism, what would it be?

5. In small groups, discuss how you might approach a loved one who is always telling ethnic jokes to try to get them to stop. Role play possible scenarios.

Native American scouts with U.S. soldiers, 1891.

chapter seven

THE BEST SCOUTS IN THE CAVALRY

WHEN PEOPLE have been oppressed for a long time, they often turn on each other. A kind of self-hate develops in the oppressed people until they get to the point where they become oppressors themselves. There are many examples of this throughout history. Some of the best scouts used by the U.S. Cavalry in its wars against American Indians were fellow American Indians. The guards that the imprisoned Jews feared most in Nazi death camps were fellow Jews.

Why was it that the best army scouts used to track Native people were Natives themselves? Who knew best the lay of the land, the better hunting and fishing spots, the better summer and winter camps, or the better places to hide from army soldiers? Who could best communicate in the Natives' languages and know their ways?

However, who would ever think some of the guards in the Nazi death camps, where six million Jews were killed in the Holocaust, were fellow Jews? And how might the reasons that explain both— why the best scouts were Native and why some of the most feared guards were Jews—be the same?

Could it be that Native scouts wanted to be accepted by the better armed, better equipped, and numerically more powerful American army? Could it be that many of the scouts were members of enemy tribes of the Native people being pursued? Did they see the struggles as being pointless as many Native people were forced to give up their land and accept placement on reservations? Did they cooperate with the soldiers to avoid the same kind of suffering Natives who were being tracked down, herded up like cattle, starved, or killed, were going through?

MY BEAUTIFUL GRANDDAUGHTER Cyan said over lunch that sometimes she gets teased because she is dark-skinned. "Auntie says that I should say, 'It's better than being just plain vanilla.'" I closed my eyes for just a moment when she said that and turned the other way.

I closed my eyes. I was a little boy standing in a school playground and a group of town boys were teasing a Native girl about being a "squaw" and an "Injun" until she cried. I closed my eyes. I was standing among a grove of old trees at Auschwitz-Birkenau, the Nazi death camp in Poland where nearly two million Jews died at the hands of the Nazis. There is a story about a little girl who survived the gas chambers there, who was pulled from the masses of bodies by other prisoners and nursed back to health. When she was discovered by the Nazis and tried to run, she was gunned down.

I closed my eyes.

"Grandpa," she said.

And certainly the Jewish guards didn't really believe all the lies used by the Nazis as excuses to carry out the genocide of millions of Jews. Their participation as guards of fellow Jews was a means of survival, as a way to temporarily postpone their own deaths. These examples serve to highlight complicated and painful issues, and knowing what leads people to act against their own ethnic group requires knowledge of *internalized* (to make part of one's own way of thinking) oppression.

To understand internalized oppression and how it manifests itself, we need to first take apart the terms and the issues that it describes. *Oppression* occurs when someone (an individual or group) dominates, *subjugates* (enslaves), uses negative stereotypes against, or denies *liberties* (freedom) to others. Other words, like abuse, torment, brutality, and injustice, also describe oppression. The *oppressor* is the person or people responsible for the oppression.

Oppression takes many forms. Denying people the right to vote because of their race is a form of oppression. Denying qualified persons of color access to equal jobs, fair housing, equal pay for equal work, or an equal education is a form of oppression. Denying people of color opportunities to achieve the high standard of living available to and enjoyed by the majority is a form of oppression. Stereotyping (as when someone labels whole groups of

TO BE FREE

Liberation day at Dachau, a Nazi concentration camp in Germany, April 29, 1945.

people as "lazy" or "alcoholics" or "stupid") is a form of oppression. Historically, the slave trade was a form of oppression. Genocide is oppression.

Internalized oppression happens when people who are oppressed oppress themselves or others from their own group. Internalized oppression occurs when an individual or group accepts or feels powerless to stop domination from other groups or enslavement, when they begin to believe the stereotypes used against them, when they feel self-hate, or when they deny liberties to others of their group. One example is when some black, Asian, Latino, white, or Native people deny their own ethnic heritage. Another example is when a person of color who succeeds in mainstream culture is sometimes perceived as trying to be too "white" by members of his or her own ethnic group. Yet another example is when someone who is mixed-race denies a part of her or his mixed heritage.

Anyone who is being abused is oppressed. When an individual who is being abused begins to believe the abuse is his or her fault (even when he or she knows deep down that it is not), this is an example of internalized oppression. Sometimes this leads to self-abuse. When this happens, the person who has been abused or oppressed tries to destroy him or herself by doing harmful things,

such as drinking too much or doing drugs. In some American Indian communities the problems with alcohol and the unusually high rates of suicide are examples of internalized oppression.

Internalized oppression manifests itself in different ways, which we'll discuss in the next few pages, including:

WHITE AS RIGHT
THE FEAR OF FREEDOM
DENYING A PART OF ONESELF
THE CRAB BUCKET
SELF-OPPRESSION

White as Right

The everyday world of a person of color is filled with subtle and not-so-subtle messages that say mainstream culture is better than their culture. For example, standardized English is used everywhere in American society—schools, businesses, and government. The language of a person of a different ethnic background, if it is used at all, may be confined to his or her home, neighborhood, or to religious ceremonies. Through the mass media (television, radio, newspapers, magazines, the Internet) young people assimilate into mainstream culture, adopting the music, dress, and values of mainstream society. Values such as *individualism* (doing your own thing), *pragmatism* (doing what is useful), *materialism* (having lots of stuff), and mainstream notions of beauty that focus on white features sometimes conflict with their traditional values. And because black, Native, Latino, and Asian history, music, literature, philosophy, and culture are often treated in brief units of study in most schools, if at all, young people of color might begin to think their ethnic heritage isn't valued. In this way, their history, culture, and ways may be lost. Tunisian-born writer Albert Memmi wrote:

> We should ask that he draws less and less from his past.... Let us ask the colonized [the oppressed] himself: who are his folk heroes? His great popular leaders? His sages? At most, he may be able to give us a few names, in complete disorder, and fewer and fewer as one goes down the generations.[30]

Some people of color may begin believing their ethnic heritage is not as good as being white. Sometimes people have even gone so far as to have plastic surgery to look white.

The fear of freedom

Those who are abused in any way are at high risk of becoming abusers themselves. Why is this? Wouldn't it seem that anyone who has been abused would work hard to ensure that they not become like the very person they once feared, dreaded, or *loathed* (hated, couldn't stand)? Unfortunately, that is not always the case. Some who have been oppressed take on some of the behaviors of their oppressors. Paulo Freire, a Brazilian educator known for his writing on oppression, wrote that "their ideal is to be men [or women]; but for them, to be men [women] is to be the oppressor. This is their model of humanity." He goes on to say that while oppressed people want to be free of oppression they may view part of their freedom as being able to be oppressors themselves. Freire calls it the "fear of freedom." The fear of freedom means that to be free is to be an oppressor.

Freire's beliefs manifest themselves in national behavior as well. Many early colonists to America came here because they were *persecuted* (discriminated against) for their religious beliefs, and found religious freedom in the new colonies. Some of these same people, however, denied religious freedom to Native people because Native beliefs were so different from their own. Others came to America because in many countries of Europe, the poor were treated much like slaves, working very low-paying jobs that kept them in a lifetime of extreme poverty. Yet, some of these same people, once they established themselves in America, supported slavery and sometimes owned slaves themselves.

World War II poster advocating Four Freedoms.

We see similar examples of this "fear of freedom" in some poor countries where revolution after revolution, or election after election, take place, each one meant to overthrow a dictator who oppresses the people. The new government establishes itself, promising new freedoms, and then begins to *repress* (stifle, outlaw) individual freedoms. So the people rise again and overthrow the new government, or vote it out of office, only to replace it with new dictators.

Paulo Freire uses a story about a peasant who becomes boss as an example of fear of freedom:

> It is a rare peasant who, once "promoted" to overseer, does not become more of a tyrant toward his former comrades [co-workers] than the owner himself. This is because the context of the peasant's situation, that is, oppression, remains unchanged. In this example, the overseer, in order to make sure of his job, must be as tough as the owner—and more so.[31]

The "fear of freedom" is difficult to understand for many of us because we live in a country where we sometimes take our freedoms for granted. We cannot imagine living in a country without basic freedoms of speech, press, or religion. So it is difficult to understand when our government promotes democracy in other nations, and some-

times these new democracies have a great deal of difficulty remaining democratic.

How can individuals, groups, and nations overcome the "fear of freedom" that is so characteristic of internalized oppression? Only when those who are oppressed recognize the causes of their oppression, confront whatever it is that oppresses them (be it racism, abuse, or whatever), and *recognize the oppressor in themselves and their own behavior*, can they transform themselves by casting out the oppression. Freire says that the first step to liberation is to confront one's own self, to look oneself in the mirror. That is where the struggle to be free begins. To be truly free is to cast out the desire to be an oppressor. Someone who is truly free would never abuse, enslave, or deprive anyone of any freedoms he or she already enjoyed.

δenying a part of oneself

Young people who are of mixed race choose which part of their background to identify with. For the most part, they identify with the ethnicity of the person who takes care of them (usually their mother): "I'm black and Native American, but as far as I'm concerned, I identify with being black." To believe that is to have a healthy self-identity. However, another person of mixed race may reject a part of their identity that is white, black, Native, Asian, or Latino. This sometimes leads to feelings of loneliness,

The Civil Rights March on Washington in 1963.

chapter eight

TO BE FREE

IN MAY 1963, the black children of Birmingham, Alabama, marched for civil rights. They came to the Sixteenth Street Baptist Church in small groups at first, but soon their numbers grew as whole classrooms, whole schools, emptied. They came by the hundreds, then the thousands. Just after noon on the first day they stepped out of the church in groups of fifty. Across the street, in Kelly Ingram Park, were the Birmingham police. By the end of the first day, 973 of the children had been arrested for unlawful gathering. Another 1,922 were arrested on day two. The police turned fire hoses on them. By day three, 4,133 were arrested. Police set their attack dogs on them.

Through it all, the children kept singing.

"Freedom! Free-dom! Free-dom! Free-dom!"

One brave little girl said that her momma told her not to go to the march. Her mother was worried she would be hurt, or worse.

"I was taught never to say no to my mother," she said. "I hear you," she told her mother. "I did not tell her I would not go. I told her, I hear you."

And the girl's voice and the voices of the children of Birmingham were heard. As a result of the march, government-sanctioned racial segregation as it had been practiced for years in Birmingham was dismantled. The victory of the children of Birmingham led to the March on Washington later in 1963, where Dr. Martin Luther King, Jr. delivered a speech that will forever be the rally cry for all those fighting for freedom, "I Have a Dream." Soon after the children's march, President John F. Kennedy introduced the bill that would become the Civil Rights Act of 1964.

WHEN I WAS YOUNG there was a group of Native kids who didn't identify with being Native. They would tell their white friends they were French Canadian or Italian or whatever, and of course they wouldn't even look at us regular rez folk. We all knew (all of us Natives, anyway) who they were because we knew their parents, grandparents, aunties, or uncles. I don't know how the rest of the regular rezers (Natives who live on the rez) felt about them, but I really resented those who didn't identify.

I carried all this resentful baggage with me into adulthood. When being Native became cool during the cultural and spiritual renaissance of the 1960s, Native people came out of the woodwork, so to speak, including most of the former "French Canadians" and "Italians." I think I resented them even more because they seemed to take all the best jobs in the reservation bureaucracy, or suddenly became cultural experts, telling everyone what was Native and what was not. Some became spokespersons for Native people to primarily non-Native audiences, and to many whites I suppose they were seen as model "Native Americans."

It took me fifty years, but now, however, I have finally grown up. I don't resent them anymore. Nor do I feel sorry for them because they spent so much time with a confused identity, or because they missed all those years being Native. I think that maybe a long time ago, back when we were all kids, being Native was just too painful for them, and sometimes people have to do whatever it takes just to survive—even if it means denying their Native heritage. So they gathered up what was Native about them and stored it away somewhere. Then one day they realized a part of their identity was missing, so they went into the hiding place and dug it out and put it on, and found themselves in the process. And they were finally free to be who they really are. I can only imagine how liberating that moment must have been.

To be free at last.

It has been more than forty years since the Children's March and Dr. King's speech on the Mall in Washington. President Kennedy was assassinated in November 1963, only five months after his civil rights bill was delivered to Congress. Dr. King was assassinated in 1968.

But the song for freedom is still being sung. In every child who hungers, in all who suffer from abuse in all its forms, in the aged who waste away in nursing homes, in the mentally ill who live homeless on the streets of our cities, in every poor neighborhood and on every Indian reservation, in every young girl exploited and oppressed by a society that begrudgingly accepts her equal role, in every war-ravaged village in a world torn apart by hatred and fear. The song for freedom is still being sung.

James Baldwin once wrote, "Not everything that is faced can be changed. But nothing can be changed until it is faced."[32]

a Beginning place

"When I despair," Mahatma Gandhi once said, "I remember that all through history the ways of truth and love have always won. There have been tyrants and murderers, and for a time they can seem invincible, but in the end they always fail. Think of it. Always."

Nelson Mandela, who fought to end Apartheid in South Africa, beneath a photograph of Mahatma Gandhi. Gandhi led the successful non-violent independence movement to free India from British control in 1947. Gandhi's philosophy of peaceful resistance inspired the American Civil Rights Movement, led by Dr. Martin Luther King, Jr.

Powpow at Mash-ka-wisen in Sawyer, Minnesota, August, 2007.

that not all whites are racists. Racism throughout history and today is not the fault of all white males, for example. This perception is false, racist, and oppressive—the very things we are working to change. In this way, we all learn from each other. Yolanda Flores Niemann, Professor of Comparative Ethnic Studies, talked about educating others:

White students learn about black students' anger at white privilege; black students learn about young whites' frustrations at being

TO BE FREE

blamed for racism beyond their control. Latinas/os learn about and talk about pride in their indigenous heritage, coupled with red, white and blue Americanism.[35]

We need to help make people of mixed race proud of their mixed heritage and to feel supported by everyone. Everyone.

We need to work hard to change the misperception in our society that we are treated equally and have equal access to opportunity. We are not yet all equal and we do not all have equal opportunity. The anti-racism work we do will help change our society to one where we will all be equal and have equal opportunity. But we are not there yet.

We need to remind ourselves that the horrors of racist and ethnic oppression are not over, not by a long shot. We need to correct the belief some hold that racial and ethnic atrocities are found only in the past: the Nazi genocide of the Jews during World War II, the genocide of Native people throughout the Americas during European colonization, the internment of Japanese Americans during World War II, and the enslavement of black people. *Ethnic cleansing* (the elimination or removal of an entire ethnic group from a region) has occurred recently—in Bosnia, and in Sudan.

We need to work actively to ensure that every school's curriculum includes voices from all ethnic backgrounds in the telling of the American story, in all subject areas—English, social studies, science, mathematics, music, and art. And we need to ensure that this is done throughout our education, from preschool through high school and college.

Participants in the Concordia University's Hmong Culture and Language Program in St. Paul.

We are all related.

TO BE FREE

We need to believe we can change the world. And then we need to do something to change it.

Finally, and most important, we need to remind ourselves that all of us share a common mother, *ni-mama aki* (Mother Earth). We are all related.

The great diversity of plants and animals on earth is inseparable from the others in a web of life. Every blade of grass, all manner of trees and flowers in their vast array of colors and smells and sizes, are related to all other plants and animals. All of the squirrels that have ever lived, all of the fish, frogs, beavers, bears, moose, and deer, all the birds in all their colors and sizes and songs—all are related to the others. All of the crawling and flying insects, grubs and worms, snakes, lizards and salamanders are our relatives.

And our closest relatives of all are our fellow humans. We come in all sizes and colors, speak many languages, and have our own unique ways of being, yet we are one *species*: human. We are one race: human.

WE ARE ALL RELATED!

CHAPTER UNDERSTANDINGS

THEME
☞ **Preventing and alleviating racism** in all its forms must involve the combined efforts of everyone: individuals, schools, communities, and nations.

ACTIVITIES TO PROMOTE UNDERSTANDING

1. Change begins with us. Do the self-assessment activity recommended early in the chapter, "My Personal Beliefs about Racism." Write down your beliefs, why you think the way you think, and the things you need to change or action you need to take.

2. Do a Web search or order some of the free video and written materials on racism from the Southern Poverty Law Center (www.teachingtolerance.org) to help begin talking about racism with others and about what can be done in your school, community, and the nation. Remember, however, that talk can only get us so far. Taking action requires courage. Be courageous.

i have a dream

BY DR. MARTIN
LUTHER KING, JR.

A portion of Dr. Martin Luther King, Jr.'s famous
"I Have a Dream" speech delivered in Washington, D. C. on August 28th, 1963:

I HAVE A DREAM that one day this nation will rise up and live out the true meaning of its creed: "We hold these truths to be self-evident: that all men are created equal." I have a dream that one day on the red hills of Georgia the sons of former slaves and the sons of former slaveowners will be able to sit down together at a table of brotherhood. I have a dream that one day even the state of Mississippi, a desert state, sweltering with the heat of injustice and oppression, will be transformed into an oasis of freedom and justice. I have a dream that my four little children will one day live in a nation where they will not be judged by the color of their skin but by the content of their character. I have a dream today....

I have a dream that one day, down in Alabama, with its vicious racists, with its governor having his lips dripping with the words of interposition and nullification, will be transformed into a situation where little black boys and black girls will be able to join hands with little white boys and white girls and walk together as sisters and brothers. I have a dream today. I have a dream that one day every valley shall be exalted, every hill and mountain shall be made low, the rough places will be made plain, and the crooked places will be made straight, and the glory of the Lord shall be revealed, and all flesh shall see it together. This is our hope. This is the faith with which I return to the South. With this faith we will be able to hew out of the mountain of despair a stone of hope. With this faith we will be able to transform the jangling discords of our nation into a beautiful

Dr. Martin Luther King, Jr. delivering his speech on the steps
of the Lincoln Memorial in Washington, D.C., on August 28, 1963.

symphony of brotherhood. With this faith we will be able to work together, to pray together, to struggle together, to go to jail together, to stand up for freedom together, knowing that we will be free one day.

This will be the day when all of God's children will be able to sing with a new meaning, "My country, 'tis of thee, sweet land of liberty, of thee I sing. Land where my fathers died, land of the pilgrim's pride, from every mountainside, let freedom ring." And if America is to be a great nation, this must become true. So let freedom ring from the prodigious hilltops of New Hampshire. Let freedom ring from the mighty mountains of New York. Let freedom ring from the heightening Alleghenies of Pennsylvania! Let freedom ring from the snow-

capped Rockies of Colorado! Let freedom ring from the curvaceous peaks of California! But not only that; let freedom ring from Stone Mountain of Georgia! Let freedom ring from Lookout Mountain of Tennessee! Let freedom ring from every hill and every molehill of Mississippi. From every mountainside, let freedom ring.

When we let freedom ring, when we let it ring from every village and every hamlet, from every state and every city, we will be able to speed up that day when all of God's children, black men and white men, Jews and Gentiles, Protestants and Catholics, will be able to join hands and sing in the words of the old Negro spiritual, **"Free at last! Free at last! Thank God Almighty, we are free at last!"**

NOTES

CHAPTER 1

1. Syracuse University. "All of Us Are Related; Each of Us is Unique." Syracuse University. http://allrelated.syr.edu/fulltext.html
2. Ibid.
3. A. Montague, *Man's Most Dangerous Myth*, 1997, p. 121
4. T. Peacock and M. Wisuri, *The Four Hills of Life*, 2006, p. 16
5. S. Molnar, *Human Variation: Races, Types, and Ethnic Groups*, 1998, p. 5
6. P. Harvey, "A Servant of Servants Shall He Be: The Construction of Race in American Religious Mythologies", in *Religion and the Creation of Race and Ethnicity*, 2003, p. 17
7. Montagu, 1997, p. 47

CHAPTER 2

8. B. Tatum, *Why Are All the Black Kids Sitting Together in the Cafeteria?*, 1997, p. 54-55
9. B. Cruz, *Multiethnic Teens and Cultural Identity*, 2001, p. 7
10. R.G. McRoy and E.M. Freeman, "Racial Identity Issues Among Mixed-Race Children" in *Social Work in Education 8*, 1986, p. 164-174
11. A. Bergstrom, L. Cleary, and T. Peacock, *The Seventh Generation*, 2003, p. 31
12. B. Cruz, 2001, p. 16
13. Ibid., p. 41

CHAPTER 3

14. H. Zinn, 1980, p. 7
15. Ibid.
16. Ibid., p. 16
17. Ibid., p. 28

18. Ibid.
19. Ibid., p. 407
20. K. Carley, *The Great Sioux Uprising of 1862*, 1976, p.1
21. J. Neidhardt, *Black Elk Speaks*, 1975, p. 262
22. M. Fedo, *The Lynchings in Duluth*, 2000, p. 106–107

CHAPTER 4

23. B. Tatum, 1997, p. 3

CHAPTER 5

24. Bergstrom, Cleary, and Peacock, 2003, p. 44
25. B. Tatum, 2003, p. 5
26. B. Tatum, 2006, http://teacher.scholastic.com/products/instructor/raceissues.htm

CHAPTER 6

27. D. Sweet, "Indian war", in Yukhita-latuhse *(she tells us stories)*, 2005, p. 40.
28. N. Butcher, in *Everyday Acts of Racism*, 1996, p. 14
29. Bergstrom, Cleary, and Peacock, 2003, p. 45

CHAPTER 7

30. A. Memmi, *The Colonizer and the Colonized*, 1965, p. 102–103
31. P. Freire, *Pedagogy of the Oppressed*, 1973, p. 30-31

CHAPTER 8

32. James Baldwin, in B. Tatum, 1997, xix
33. M. Roth, in *Everyday Acts of Racism*, 1996, p. 11
34. N. Butcher, 1996, p. 18
35. Y. Neimann, in *Everyday Acts of Racism*, 1996, p. 38

SELECTED BIBLIOGRAPHY

Barnett, S.A. *The Human Species*. New York: Harper and Row, 1971.

Benton-Banai, Edward. *The Mishomis Book*. Hayward, Wisconsin: Indian Country Communications, 1988.

Bergstrom, Amy, Linda Miller Cleary, and Thomas D. Peacock. *The Seventh Generation*. Charleston, West Virginia: ERIC Clearinghouse on Rural Education & Small, 2003.

Brendtro, Larry K., Martin Brokenleg, and Steve Van Bockern. *Reclaiming Youth at Risk*. Bloomington, Indiana: National Education Service, 1992.

Butcher, Nancy. "Undoing the Smile," in *Everyday Acts Against Racism: Raising Children in a Multiracial World*, ed. Maureen Reddy (Seattle, Washington: Seal Press, 1996), 12-20.

Carley, Kenneth. *The Dakota War of 1862*. St. Paul, Minnesota: Minnesota Historical Society Press, 2001.

Cleary, Linda Miller, and Thomas D. Peacock. *Collected Wisdom: American Indian Education*. Needham Heights, Massachusetts: Allyn and Bacon, 1998.

Coon, Carleton. *The Story of Man*. 3rd ed. New York: Alfred A. Knopf, 1969.

Cowan, D. "Theorizing Race: The Construction of Christian Identity," in *Religion and the Creation of Race and Ethnicity*, ed. Craig Prentiss (New York: New York University Press, 2003), 112-123.

Cruz, Barbara C. *Multiethnic Teens and Cultural Identity*. Berkeley Heights, New Jersey: Enslow Publishers, 2001.

Fedo, Michael. *The Lynchings in Duluth*. St. Paul, Minnesota: Minnesota Historical Society Press, 2000.

Freeman, E.M. and R.G. McRoy. "Racial Identity Issues Among Mixed-Race Children." *Social Work in Education 8* (1986): 164-174.

Freire, Paulo. *Pedagogy of the Oppressed*. New York: The Seabury Press, 1973.

Harvey, Paul. "A Servant of Servants Shall He Be: The Construction of Race in American Religious Mythologies," in *Religion and the Creation of Race and Ethnicity*, ed. Craig Prentiss (New York: New York University Press, 2003), 13-27.

Memmi, Albert. *The Colonizer and the Colonized*. New York: The Orion Press, 1965.

Molnar, Stephen. *Human Variation: Races, Types, and Ethnic Groups*. Upper Saddle River, New Jersey: Prentice-Hall, 1998.

Montagu, Ashley. *Man's Most Dangerous xMyth*. Walnut Creek, California: SAGE Publications, 1997.

Neidhardt, John. *Black Elk Speaks*. 1932. Reprint ed. New York: Pocket Books, 1975.

Neimann, Yolanda Flores. "Nurturing Antiracism," in *Everyday Acts Against Racism: Raising Children in a Multiracial World*, ed.

Maureen Reddy (Seattle, Washington: Seal Press, 1996), 31-39.

Peacock, Thomas, and Marlene Wisuri. *Ojibwe: Waasa Inaabidaa*. Afton, Minnesota: Afton Historical Society Press, 2002.

Peacock, Thomas, and Marlene Wisuri. *The Four Hills of Life*. Afton, Minnesota: Afton Historical Society Press, 2006.

Roth, Martha. "You Have to Start Somewhere," in *Everyday Acts Against Racism: Raising Children in a Multiracial World*, ed. Maureen Reddy (Seattle, Washington: Seal Press, 1996), 3-12.

Sapp, Jeff. *Mighty Times: The Children's March*. Montgomery, Alabama: Southern Poverty Law Center, 2005.

Sproul, Barbara C. *Primal Myths*. New York: Harper and Row, 1979.

Sweet, Denise. "Indian war," in Yukhitalatuhse *(she tells us stories)*. Green Bay, Wisconsin: Oneida Nation Arts Program, 2005. Reprinted by permission of the author.

Tatum, Beverly Daniel, Ph.D. *Why Are All the Black Kids Sitting Together in the Cafeteria?* 1997. Reprint ed. New York: Basic Books, 2003.

Tiedt, Pamela L., and Iris M. Tiedt. *Multicultural Teaching*. Boston, Massachusetts: Allyn and Bacon, 2005.

Zinn, Howard. *A People's History of the United States*. New York: Harper and Row, 1980.

ILLUSTRATION CREDITS

CONCORDIA UNIVERSITY
St. Paul, Minnesota
p. 107, children, photographer
Cher Rafferty, August 9, 2007.

CORBIS CORPORATION
p. 15, Early Man Migrations map; p. 36, Barack Obama; p. 59, U.S./Mexican border, Gifford Porter; p. 76, protestors, photographer Wally McNamee, 1991.

JEFF CROSBY
New York, New York
p. 2, multiethnic face illustration.

GETTY IMAGES
p. 12, DNA strand, illustrator Imagezoo; p. 101, Ghandi and Mandela, photography by P. MUSTAFA/AFP, October 15, 1990.

ICONOGRAPHIC ENCYCLOPEDIA: HISTORY AND ETHNOLOGY
New York, New York
p. 20, engraving of racial types, Rudolph Garrigue, 1851.

ISTOCK PHOTO
www.istockphoto.com
p. 6, children with flag; p. 9, jump for joy; p. 10, circle of hands; p. 34, couple; p. 96, concentration camp; p. 115, kids.

LEPAGE PHOTOGRAPHY
Superior, Wisconsin
p. 102, medical students, photographer Roger LePage.

LIBRARY OF CONGRESS
Washington, D.C.
p. 17, Eskimo man; p. 18, fountain; p. 22, slave poster; p. 38, Christopher Columbus; p. 43, slave auction, engraving by Theodore R. Davis, 1861; p. 44, Abraham Lincoln, artist Jean Louis Gerome Ferris, 1863-1930; p. 45, Japanese detainee, photographer Dorothea Lange, April 1942; p. 46, Manzanar camp, photographer Ansel Adams, 1943; p. 57, Founding Fathers, designer Terry Robbins, watercolor, ink; p. 81, Japanese girl, photographer Ansel Adams, Library of Congress, 1943; p. 86, Lakota scouts, photographer John C. H. Grabill, 1891; p. 92, Works Progress Administration Poster Collection; p. 98, March on Washington, photographer Warren K. Leffler, August 1963.

MINNESOTA HISTORICAL SOCIETY
St. Paul, Minnesota
p. 26, Nett Lake, photographer Monroe P. Killy, September 1, 1946; p. 49, Sioux captives, photographer Adrian J. Ebell, arte-de-visite, 1862; p. 50, Medicine Man, photography by Northwestern Photo Co.; p. 54, porter, 1935; p. 66, boarding school; p. 67, Temple Israel, ca. 1890; p. 73, Martin Luther King, Jr., photography by St. Paul Pioneer Press, April 27, 1967; p. 83, Ku Klux Klan, September 1922.

PRIVATE COLLECTION
p. 111, Martin Luther King, Jr.

SCALA / ART RESOURCES
New York, New York
p. 71, Head of Cleopatra, artist Michelangelo Buonarroti, Casa Buonarroti, Florence, Italy.

TRACY SENECA
Oakland, California
p. 58, sign.

UNITED STATES HOLOCAUST MEMORIAL MUSEUM
Washington, D.C.
p. 64, Star of David patch, courtesy of Charles and Hana Bruml; p. 89, Dachau, courtesy of National Archives and Records Administration.

MARLENE WISURI
Duluth, Minnesota
p. 16, desert plant; p. 24, hands; p. 29, race exhibit; p. 33, advertising example; p. 41, Nina protest; p. 47, Sandy Lake monument; p. 51, memorial; p. 62, memorial; p. 63, interpreter; p. 70, Japanese art; p. 74, playground; p. 84, memorial; p. 106, pow-wow.

TOU GER XIONG
Woodbury, Minnesota
p. 105, Hmong comedian, photographer Shila Yang.

this Book was designed
with care By

Mary Susan Oleson
NASHVILLE, TENNESSEE